A State of Opportunity

A plan to build a healthier, smarter, stronger,

younger, and more prosperous Maine

Eliot Cutler

Published in the State of Maine, United States by The Atlantica Press
Printed on recycled paper

ISBN: 978-0-9849949-3-9

To download a copy of A State of Opportunity,
visit our website at www.EliotCutler.com

Photography Credits in Alphabetical Order:
Kevin Morris - page 38 (solar panels)
soggy dog designs - pages 38 (ship), 43, 94
Michele Stapleton - pages 6, 8, 24, 29, 104
Dennis Welsh - page 38 (kayak and snow play)

Authorized by the Candidate and paid for by Cutler for Maine.
P.O. Box 17766 • Portland, Maine 04112
207-358-7000 • info@eliotcutler.com

Full color copies of this book can be downloaded at www.eliotcutler.com

This book is for Melanie Stewart Cutler,

whose saintly patience and abiding love

have sustained me for 40 years.

Acknowledgments

After my 2010 campaign for governor, an interviewer asked me whether I had any regrets. I told her that my only regret was that I lost – and that single regret, I said, was dwarfed by the profoundly wonderful experience of making new friendships with thousands of Maine people.

I have learned the most from, and owe my greatest debt to, the good people of Maine. For more than four years now they have invited me into their homes and businesses and have shared with me their hopes and dreams – for themselves, for their families and for the State of Maine. Thank you to each and every one of them.

No campaign is possible without hundreds of dedicated volunteers and thousands of contributors, and I must acknowledge and thank each of them again for their trust in me, their support for the effort that we have undertaken together, and for their confidence that we will prevail.

I have thought about how to overcome Maine's challenges and how to create opportunity for Maine people for most of my life. Scores of wise and generous people have informed and taught me along the way. They all have helped – wittingly or unwittingly – to shape my thinking and have contributed in ways large and small to the plan set out in this book. There is no satisfactory way – and my memory is inadequate – to thank each of them again here. I remain deeply grateful to all of them.

There are a few people, though, whom I must acknowledge in particular and by name:

It is impossible for me to overstate the importance of the examples set – and the opportunities created – for me by my grandfather Harry Epstein and by my parents Catherine and Lawrence Cutler. I was lucky. I won a genetic lottery when I was born to them in Bangor, Maine in 1946. I feel driven every day by my obligation to square the books and to repay the debt my family and I owe to Maine and to the people of Maine.

The greatest teacher I ever had was Senator Edmund S. Muskie, and so the similarities between his political values and mine are no accident. I have borrowed from him the touchstones of broad opportunity, fiscal discipline, and the vigilant protection of public health and environmental quality. I have sought to practice, as he did, the arts of collaboration and patient, persistent persuasion.

Perry Newman was alternately my muse and seer in writing this book. Ted O'Meara has been my friend for 50 years and my closest partner and counselor for nearly five. Betts Gorsky has helped me collect my own thoughts, collected those of many others, and contributed many of her own. Cara Brown McCormick has provided exceptional research and editing assistance. I could not have conceived the elements of the plan nor completed the book without copious amounts of help and advice from Perry, Ted, Betts and Cara.

Whitney Campbell and Ben Schmidt lent their considerable talents to the graphics and to the book's design and publication.

My wife Melanie, our children Abby and Zack and my brothers Josh and Joel have strong convictions and ideas of their own, particularly regarding health care, and these are reflected in important ways throughout this book.

I am grateful to all of these people, and to so many more, for their input, ideas, patience and creativity. They are in many ways responsible for what is good and correct in this book.

It goes without saying, therefore, that any errors, inconsistencies or inaccuracies herein are solely my responsibility.

Table of Contents

Introduction
Not Left... Not Right... *Forward!*

- Maine is a great place to live but it's a hard place to make a living.

- Many of our challenges are the result of bad choices and failed policies.

- Mainers want leaders to focus on solutions, not on scoring political points.

- Maine needs a new vision, a new plan and a new strategy that inspires us to invest in our competitive advantages and maximizes opportunity.

Maine is an exceptional place.

Anyone who has visited our state – even for only a short time – knows that it just doesn't get much better than this. From Eastport to Eustis, from Kittery to Fort Kent, our rocky coast, our mountains, rivers, lakes, farms and fields all bear witness to the fact that Maine is not only the most beautiful state in America, it is one of the most beautiful places *anywhere.*

Those of us who are lucky enough to live here know that what makes Maine much more than just pretty postcards are Maine people. Basic decency, independence, a dogged work ethic, and an abiding commitment to civility are the underpinnings of our remarkable statewide community.

That Maine community allowed my grandparents and my parents to raise a family not only in a place of beauty, but also – and most important – in a place of economic opportunity.

Those of us who make Maine our home, though, know that however great a place Maine is to live, for too many Mainers it's not a great place to make a living. Maine has been mired in economic doldrums for more than a decade, and too many Maine people suffer from a lack of opportunity.

The remedy for this chronic underperformance begins with what we can do for ourselves and for each other, but we also need to have a serious conversation about what

1

ought to be our state government's role in curing our economic ills – and then we need to get about the business of doing it right.

It's *all* about opportunity. Our politics *ought* to be about making sure that everyone in Maine has it.

It's not for lack of initiative, or creativity, or natural resources that Maine people earn less than our neighbors in New Hampshire, Vermont or, indeed, *anywhere* in New England. It's not for lack of good universities, renowned researchers or dedicated teachers. It's not even the absence of large population centers that explains our lower earnings and reduced economic mobility.

Maine has fallen behind because we have not responded to our economic and social challenges in smart and strategic ways. Too many of our current challenges are the consequence of bad choices and the fruit of failed policies.

Maine's economy is stuck, with no more non-farm jobs in January, 2013[1] than in October, 1999 and incomes that aren't keeping pace with the rest of the country.

- Yet we have failed to reform a tax structure that is unfair, inhibits growth and spends hundreds and hundreds of million dollars in tax giveaways every year without sufficient review by the governor or the legislature.[2]

- We have failed to make capital investments that would protect and leverage our competitive advantages – even though the ratio of *per capita debt* to *per capita GDP* is the lowest in New England and lower than the average among all states[3] and even though interest rates have been at record lows.

- And we have failed to build a Maine brand that would yield higher prices for Maine's quality products, including our tourist experience.

Even as callous state policies bar access to preventive health care for thousands of Maine citizens, a greater and greater percentage of our state revenues is gobbled up by health care and related program costs.

---

[1] Maine Department of Labor, Center for Workforce Research and Information, and U.S. Bureau of Labor Statistics.

[2] In the 126th Maine Legislature (adjourned, July 1, 2013) Sen. Emily Cain and Rep. Peggy Rotundo, recognizing the lingering fiscal impacts of this lack of oversight, jointly sponsored L.D. 1488, which required the Committee on Taxation to recommend which tax expenditure programs would be kept, repealed or changed, and would thereafter require full legislative action in an up or down vote as part of the budget process. Rep. Peter Stuckey advocated requiring the state to develop mechanisms for evaluating the effectiveness of tax expenditures. These are sensible approaches that I first recommended in 2010, and still strongly support.

[3] www.usgovernmentspending.com

• Yet we have failed to reform Maine's health care system, which suffers from high costs, poor oversight and an overreliance on health insurance companies whose premiums have become more and more unaffordable for Maine businesses and individuals.

• And we have failed to invest in the kinds of initiatives – ranging from preventive health care to early childhood education – that we *know* would bend the curve and lower Maine's health care costs.

Maine's national leadership position in public education has been squandered, and we are losing too many of our young people to other states – a process that reinforces our demographic challenge and accelerates our economy's downward spiral.

• Yet we have failed to stabilize state funding for public schools. Instead, we have shifted the funding burden to local property taxes, leaving communities not only short of what they were promised, but in many cases stretched beyond their limits. We rely excessively, as a result, on highly regressive local property taxes. That is inequitable, and it denies opportunity to far too many Maine children.

• We have failed to reform and re-structure preK-12 education in ways that will reward good teachers, encourage innovation, and provide incentives for cost-effective collaboration among cities, towns and school districts.

• And we have failed to put in place a program of early childhood education that virtually every ounce of available data indicates will save Mainers hundreds of millions of dollars.

Even though Maine's students graduate from secondary school at among the highest rates in the country, too few go on to study and to acquire employable skills in our universities and community colleges.

• Yet we have permitted tuitions at Maine's colleges and universities to become some of the highest in America and have failed to merge the governance of two competing systems that remain uncoordinated and don't offer students clear enough paths to two-year and four-year degrees.

Perhaps Maine's biggest single challenge is our age. In short, we're too old. Maine's population is the oldest in the country and is aging more quickly than the rest of the nation.

3

• Yet we have failed to develop and pursue a plan to make Maine younger – by taking steps, for example, to attract young, skilled college graduates and immigrants who will start farms and businesses, employ other Mainers and help Maine's economy grow again.

There are so many things right with Maine that we have no business accepting these circumstances as givens. Our lives and our children's futures don't have to be, and shouldn't be, limited by the mistakes that have been made in the past. Those mistakes can be corrected. Our problems can be solved. Our challenges *can* be met.

When we make real progress on our critical challenges, it will mean the difference between stagnation and growth for Maine's economy, between poverty and prosperity for many of Maine's citizens, between hopelessness and opportunity for Maine's youth.

What stands in our way is simply the fact that the State of Maine has no plan for Maine's future, no road map by which to guide decision after decision of critical importance to Maine people.

In part this is because our politics are broken. Even though we all recognize that Maine faces severe tests, it has been nearly impossible to move the needle in our polarized political environment. Our ability to engage in public discourse – to explore together the very solutions and strategies that might benefit Maine and to make hard choices together – has fallen victim to bitter partisanship that has divided our community. Many of our leaders have come to look at politics, and at governing itself, as a zero-sum, winner-take-all, blood sport. In that sort of environment, sound solutions to difficult and complex public problems – best developed in an environment of collaboration and compromise – not only are hard to come by, they are nearly impossible to implement.

When an acrimonious political environment takes hold in a state like ours that already is challenged by an aging population, an expensive infrastructure, a fragile tax base and high health care and education costs, the consequences can be widespread social and economic jeopardy.

Far too much time and energy has been wasted by distracting political sideshows and needless brinkmanship. Maine people have told me clearly – over and over again – that they don't want to live in a "my way or the highway" environment; they don't want their leaders to engage in the kind of partisanship that encourages all-or-nothing politics; they don't want Augusta to fall victim to the hyper-partisan divides that have paralyzed Washington.

Overwhelmingly, Mainers want their leaders to focus on solutions, not on scoring political points. Maine people want their leaders to shed destructive, scorched earth tactics and to devote their energies instead to seeking common ground, finding solutions, and working collaboratively for the benefit of Maine people. Maine people want leaders with the kind of temperament that leads to forward progress and good results.

Maine people deserve leaders who understand the complexity of our problems; who are rational and examine facts without rancor; who are willing to engage in honest and meaningful dialogue; and who are capable of crafting and implementing a strategic plan that serves the interests of Maine citizens.

I suffer from few illusions. I know that it won't be easy to fashion and to put in place a coherent plan for solving Maine's problems and rebuilding our economy. But lurching from one crisis to another without having anticipated the crises and without having developed a strategy to overcome them – which is where we are now and where we've been for more than a decade – certainly is a poor substitute for a plan.

I know from my own experience in business and government that a good plan can be developed and *will* be embraced and implemented if it is the product of clear vision, honest dialogue, widespread input and meaningful collaboration.

A plan for Maine doesn't need to be red or blue, right or left, liberal or conservative. It needs to be smart and to stand on the facts. It needs to protect and to create opportunities for each Maine citizen to reach his or her greatest potential. It needs to be fair and to be fiscally responsible. And it needs to be given a chance to work.

Maine will have better jobs, higher incomes and stronger economic growth when we put in place innovative strategies to reduce our health care and education costs while improving access to both; when we position our strongest and most competitive industries for greater profitability; and when we meet our own expectations for fairness, justice and faithful stewardship of our surroundings and our democracy.

So, let's take stock of our competitive advantages; let's agree on a plan for economic growth that leverages our strengths and shores up our weaknesses; and let's recommit ourselves as a community of 1,300,000 independent Mainers to the shared enterprise of rebuilding Maine's economy.

The same extraordinary qualities of our state that cause people to want to live here and to visit here are also the competitive advantages that once created great prosperity and can do so again – *but not in the same ways as before*. We won't find the answers to our challenges in a rearview mirror. We need a new vision, a plan and a strategy that points the way *forward*.

I have proposed in this book a plan and a strategy – concrete steps that I think we ought to take and that together we *can* take – that will make Maine a state where our economic opportunity equals the beauty of our surroundings. The plan is a starting point – for discussion, debate and collaboration.

I can't do it alone – no Governor can – but I stand ready to provide the leadership and commitment that can get us moving in the directions that will make Maine both a great place to live *and* a great place to make a living.

I invite you to join the discussion, help in the effort and share the reward of a more prosperous, secure and vibrant state of Maine.

PART ONE:

What Happened To Maine?

1

A Double Whammy:
The Dimensions of Our Challenge

- A double whammy: low incomes and high expenses.

- We have lagged our New England neighbors and the rest of the United States in both job creation and income.

- Our small population struggles to generate sufficient revenue to maintain the physical and social infrastructure of our state.

- The good news: we can fix it.

- Our foremost challenge is making and following a plan – to invest in Maine's future, to lower our costs of living, to increase economic activity, jobs and incomes, and to broaden opportunity.

The central premise of this book is that Maine people need and deserve considerably greater opportunity to prosper than they have today.

Opportunity means jobs, of course. But it also means more, much more.

Opportunity means better, higher-paying jobs and the education to qualify for them. The health of the Maine economy is reflected first and foremost in the number and quality of jobs. Unless ideas, policies and priorities can help to generate promising prospects for more and better jobs in the future, they are of little practical benefit and often amount to nothing more than political sloganeering.

Opportunity also means access to health care in a system that costs us less because it is well organized and managed in the public interest, and because it rewards illness prevention as much as it rewards medical procedures.

In a larger sense, opportunity means restoring a generation's confidence that our children's lives can be better than our own.

However you define it, opportunity is the secret sauce that turns possibility into prosperity.

Everything about opportunity for Maine people comes back to the health of the Maine economy. Exacerbated during the past ten years by a series of policy mistakes and missed opportunities, the challenges of technology, competition, high operating costs and stagnant and insufficient educational attainment[4] have left Maine today with a rapidly aging population, a sluggish economy, a growing gap between public needs and our ability to meet them... and less opportunity for Maine people.

Poor employment and earnings trends in Maine reflect both the impact of technology on manufacturing and the outcome of a *status quo* approach to leadership amidst a worldwide environment of dynamic change. Although technology and global competition have created in many states *both* challenges and opportunities for employers and workers, in Maine we've seen more challenges and fewer opportunities.

There are some amazing stories of innovation in Maine, but overall we have failed for the past decade to keep pace with the changes that technology and market pressures have imposed, and so, as a consequence, we have lagged our New England neighbors and the rest of the United States in both job creation and income.

The trends in jobs, output and incomes comprise the first punch in a double whammy that has hit Maine people. Rising living expenses and increasing costs of government make up the second.

It's one thing to live with incomes and a GDP that trail much of the country, but when the costs of day to day living and providing public services are also disproportionately expensive, the disconnect can become even more pronounced. If we don't take action soon, it will get so challenging to make a go of it in Maine that our population trends will look even worse than they do today.

Before we focus on what to do about it, let's first try to understand how and why we got to this toxic combination of jobs that are too few, incomes that are too low and costs that are too high.

* * *

---

4 The high school graduation rate in Maine was 85.34% in 2012, according to the Maine Department of Education, but Maine's college and university graduation rates are much too low. Only 48.5% of all Maine graduates complete a four-year degree in the first six years following their initial enrollment. According to the Chronicle of Higher Education, the rates at some Maine colleges are even lower ... much lower. See, http://collegecompletion.chronicle.com/state/#state=me&sector=public_four. In these times, access to opportunity makes post-secondary education or training not a "nice to have," but a "need to have."

Anyone who lives, works and pays taxes in Maine is aware of the challenges inherent in living here. Our population is small, and our economy is small.

Despite the challenges, though, for many Mainers life here really is the way life should be. If you own a successful business, for example; if you are fortunate enough to have a good and secure job; if you are able to pay your mortgage or make the rent; if you are in good health and are insured; if you live in a stable home environment free from risk of domestic abuse; then there are few better places to live on this earth than here in Maine.

Unfortunately, this isn't the case for many of us. If the cost of doing business in Maine is becoming prohibitive; if you are unemployed or underemployed with few prospects for advancement; if the industry in which you are employed is itself at risk; if you face illness or disease without the means to obtain good health care; if the legacy of domestic or alcohol abuse is visited upon you, and prospects for relief or escape are remote; if you are one of the thousands of Maine children who go to bed hungry every night or are unprepared to learn when you reach school age; then our state's natural beauty and welcoming communities offer limited consolation.

As a mother told her young son years ago as he marveled at the beauty of Cadillac Mountain, "Just remember, you can't eat the view."

Maine can be a very expensive place to live for anyone. Energy costs are high relative to other areas of the country, the state's infrastructure is old and costly to maintain, and Maine people pay more than our neighbors and our peers to support state and local governments that are by many measures too costly and in urgent need of an overhaul.

In fact, that's the double whammy in a nutshell: incomes are low and expenses are high. Every business understands, and every family on a budget knows, that when resources do not align with expenses, something's got to give.

The good news is that we have it within our power to change the situation, both with respect to economic performance and also with regard to the cost of governing ourselves and providing public services. Improving the economy is not a short-term project, however. It will take sound policy decisions, consistent implementation over a number of years and plain hard work to create the conditions under which Maine people will enjoy more diverse and better economic opportunities.

As for expenses, there certainly aren't any magic wands that we can wave over them to make them disappear. We *know* the areas of excessive spending and redundancy that contribute to the imbalance between incomes and expenditures. But getting to a balance, to greater stability, remains a continuing unmet challenge years after the core problems were identified and understood.

As we work to develop responses and strategies that will position Maine people for greater prosperity and security, we have to know where we are and how steep is the climb ahead of us. We'll never manage (or cure) what we can't measure.

Statistics and other quantitative indicators are an essential starting point in any reasoned discussion of Maine's current situation, whether we're talking about the costs of government, economic performance, educational attainment, or demographic trends. If the data consistently suggest that state government is spending too much or that certain segments of the Maine economy are clearly underperforming, for example, we need to consider the possibility that something really is amiss.

In the discussion that follows, therefore, the taking-off points will be, in many cases, statistics and data from a number of credible sources. We should look to this data for guidance in forming our conclusions, but we also should be informed by the realities on the ground and the real-life experiences of real Maine people and businesses.[5]

* * *

Without getting overwhelmed by the numbers, it's instructive to take a look at some of the key indicators that reflect Maine's challenges. To sum it all up:

- We're old and getting older.

- We're poor and getting poorer (relative to the rest of the country).

- Machines are getting smarter, foreign competition is getting tougher, and lots of jobs in traditional industries are likely gone for good.

- Our costs of living – health care, education, and public services – are high and getting higher.

---

[5] As Mark Twain famously observed, there are three kinds of lies: lies, damned lies, and statistics. Twain meant that statistics, for all their apparent credibility, can be manipulated to create what seem to be factual and quantifiable bases for the positions we take. Behind all of the statistics about life in Maine there is a real, tangible human component. When, for example, political leaders decide with a wave of the pen that 70,000 Mainers will be left out of MaineCare coverage, we must never forget that almost all of those people are deserving folks whom we have no right to leave behind.

• And we are responsible for a piece of real estate that is big and increasingly expensive to maintain.

Countless white papers and articles, the original Brookings Study and an important 2010 follow-on study called "Reinventing Maine Government"[6] have examined Maine's demography, economy and government. Uniformly they have warned about a looming fiscal crisis in government and a stagnant economy that discourages Maine people and limits investment.[7] Here are some of the relentless facts that support those conclusions:

• Maine is the oldest state in the country (median age in Maine, 43.5 years; median age in the US, 37.4)

• In 2012, roughly 270,000 Mainers were under eighteen, while 225,000 Mainers were over sixty-five years of age.

• In 2030, only 255,000 Mainers will be under 18, while 374,000 Mainers will be over sixty-five years of age.

• Maine is aging faster than the rest of the country. (A decade ago, the median age in Maine was 38.6 years, fourth oldest in the country; now Maine is the oldest state in the country.)

• Maine is already 49th in percentage of residents under eighteen, and 3rd in percentage of residents over sixty-five.

• Maine's population has remained virtually stagnant, at 1.3 million, for the past decade.

• Ten of Maine's sixteen counties saw more deaths than births over the past decade.

Taken together, these indicators[8] reflect an aging population that is less likely to start new businesses, less likely to generate new tax revenues long-term, more likely to be living on fixed incomes, more likely to need expensive health care and more likely to be dependent on a social safety net.

---

6 *"Reinventing Maine Government,"* © 2010, Envision Maine, available online at https://sites.google.com/site/envisionmaine/reinventing-maine-government

7 *Id.*, at p. 3.

8 Sources for the foregoing bullet points include *U.S Census Bureau, Population Division; U.S. Department of Commerce, Bureau of Economic Analysis; Bangor Daily News; University of Maine;* and *MaineBiz, 2012 Book of Lists.*

As old as we are, there also aren't very many of us, and together we're responsible for a lot of territory. With 1.3 million residents, Maine is only the 41st most populous state in the country, but we occupy a large plot of land compared with many of our more populous neighbors in the northeastern United States. Even though Maine's 31,000 square miles of territory place us only 39th in size among the fifty states, Maine is larger than all five of the other New England states combined. Unlike many of our smaller neighbors, however, the overall population density of Maine is sparse, 43 persons per square mile.

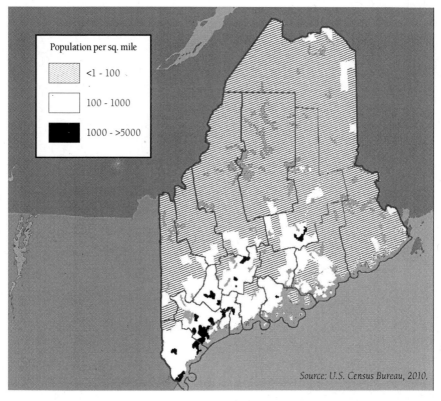

Source: U.S. Census Bureau, 2010.

Of course, Maine is not *uniformly* sparse. More than half of our population resides in a comparatively small area in the southern part of the state, generally concentrated along the coast south from Bath and Brunswick. As a result, there are extreme differences in the population and related characteristics of the different parts of our state – perhaps more pronounced differences than exist almost anywhere else in the United States.

The population density of coastal Cumberland County, Maine's most populous and densest county, is 337 persons per square mile. If Cumberland County was a state, it would rank 9th in density among all the states, just behind Florida and ahead of Pennsylvania. Yet in Piscataquis County, our least densely populated county, there are only 4.3 persons per square mile. If Piscataquis County was a state, it would rank 49th – ahead of only Alaska, and considerably less densely populated than Wyoming.

To put things in even sharper relief, the population density in Piscataquis County has hardly changed in the last fifty years, but the population density in Cumberland County has increased roughly 50% during this period.

The bottom line is that while the population of Maine as a whole has stayed largely the same for the past twenty years, the population of coastal urban areas has been growing, with certain counties becoming particularly dense, while population growth in our rural interior has been virtually non-existent. The map below dramatically reflects changes in population density over the preceding four decades:

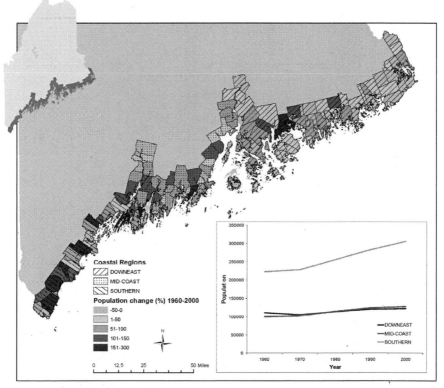

Source: Abbett and Englert, "The State of Coastal and Marine Management in Maine," Chapter 1, The State of Maine's Environment, Colby College, Environmental Policy Group, Environmental Studies Program (2009).

Our demographic and geographic burdens don't just drive the costs of social services typically accessed by older or poorer citizens. Geography, population size and age, and population density combine to present a difficult set of service and political challenges for all of us.

With a large area to manage and maintain, but with few people overall and even fewer in our most remote areas, Maine's small population struggles to generate sufficient revenue to keep up the infrastructure, physical and social, of the state. Put another way, the costs of maintaining a relatively high number of miles of roads, bridges, ports and parks, and schools, public safety officers and the demands of the social safety net, fall upon a relatively small population.

Moreover, as Maine's population and tax base age, the consequent decline in revenues supporting critical public functions will impact everyone. Maine has more than 46,000 miles of roadway to maintain, while neighboring New Hampshire, with virtually the same population, has only 33,000 miles. Then there are the bridges, the dams, the ports, the buildings and the rest of our infrastructure for which governments – state and local – are responsible.

The numbers don't lie. Unless we do something to reverse Maine's demographic trends, Maine people will be stretched beyond the breaking point; the costs of all of our public services will continue to rise further and further, while our governments' revenues – the ability to pay those costs – will decline more and more.

Regrettably, there are even more circumstances that make it discouragingly expensive to live and to do business in Maine. Take a quick look at our costs for higher education and health care.[9]

In 2011 average tuition at a two-year public college in Maine was $3,272, while average tuition at a four-year public college here was $8,018 – both roughly thirteen percent higher than the respective national averages.[10] Higher tuition costs, particularly when set alongside our incomes, likely impact our educational attainment; in 2010, 35.8% of Mainers held a higher degree, just one tenth of a percent above the national figure, and well below the 43.4% of New Englanders as a whole who hold a post-high school degree.

---

[9] Energy remains another big cost factor Between 65 and 70 percent of Maine people depend on oil to heat their homes, and as more Maine people find it difficult to pay the rising costs of oil (and propane), there is less public assistance available to help them do so. Further, the delivered residential cost of electricity in Maine in 2012 was nearly 14.47 cents per kilowatt hour, the seventh highest rate in the continental United States; and while the cost of commercial electricity in Maine is the lowest in New England, it is still higher – as much as 25% higher – than it is in states and provinces with which we compete economically.

[10] U.S. Department of Education, College Affordability and Transparency Center, http://collegecost.ed.gov/catc/

Maine health care costs were 22.4% of GDP in 2009, a full 50% higher than the average U.S. figure of 14.9% in the same year, which itself is the highest percentage of any industrialized country in the world.[11] These numbers are just the tip of the iceberg; there simply isn't any doubt that it costs a lot to live in Maine and to provide public services for Maine people.[12]

Our geographic and demographic challenges are brought into even sharper focus when we look at how much Maine people earn, and how much we earn has a lot to do with how much we produce.

Maine's gross domestic product (GDP) in 2011 was $51.6 billion, ranking Maine 42nd in the country, and Maine's *per capita* personal income[13] in 2011 was $38,299, or only 92.1% of the U.S. average, 29th among all states and last among the New England states. Our GDP hasn't been growing as fast as the rest of New England or the U.S. as a whole, and our incomes haven't either.

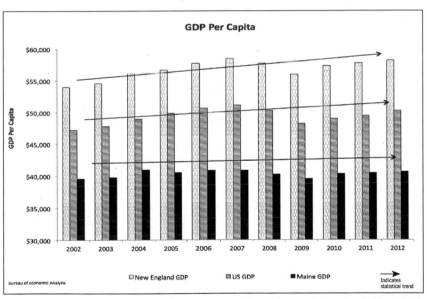

Both U.S. and New England GDP per capita have grown 0.7% annually over the last decade. The U.S. has added $3,047 in per capita GDP over that time, while New England has added $4,214.

---

[11] *Measures of Growth in Focus 2012; 2013, Maine Economic Growth Council, 2012; 2013.*

[12] It is political sophistry of the worst sort to suggest that the reason those costs are so high in comparison, say, to New Hampshire is because New Hampshire has lower taxes; indeed, that's putting the cart squarely before the horse.

[13] Personal *per capita* income is a figure widely used to measure the economic strength of a population within a given location relative to other populations. It is the income received from all sources divided by the state's population. These sources include wages, salary, supplements, rents, dividends, interest, and transfer payments to individuals for which no current services are performed, such as Social Security, unemployment, welfare assistance and veteran's benefits. (*Measures of Growth, 2013.*)

Maine has seen only a little more than half the growth as New England and the US, adding just 0.4% per year and $1,088 to *per capita* GDP in the last ten years.

The problem certainly isn't that Maine people don't work hard enough to earn higher salaries. In 2010, 7% of Maine workers held more than one job compared with only 4.9% in the United States as a whole.[14] Yet despite this industriousness, neither incomes nor state output have gained much ground on the rest of the country during the past decade. At best, we are barely keeping pace.[15]

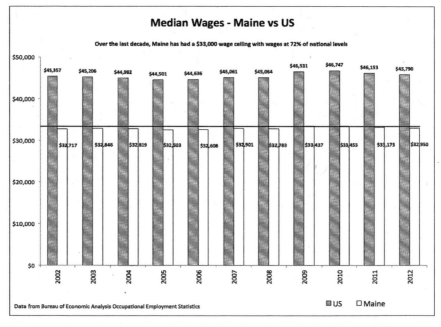

Median Wages - Maine vs US

Over the last decade, Maine has had a $33,000 wage ceiling with wages at 72% of national levels

US: $45,357, $45,206, $44,982, $44,501, $44,636, $45,061, $45,064, $46,531, $46,747, $46,153, $45,790

Maine: $32,717, $32,846, $32,819, $32,503, $32,608, $32,901, $32,783, $33,437, $33,453, $33,173, $32,950

Years: 2002, 2003, 2004, 2005, 2006, 2007, 2008, 2009, 2010, 2011, 2012

Data from Bureau of Economic Analysis Occupational Employment Statistics

■ US □ Maine

Maine's average annual wage growth over the last decade has been one-third less than the US, at 0.2% versus 0.3%

One of the reasons for the relative decline in Mainers' earnings is that big employers that once provided job stability and employment continuity, such as the shoe industry and the textile mills, no longer dominate the Maine economy. In paper and other industries where Maine people in Maine jobs once added value to Maine natural resources, technology and competition have squeezed out many employment opportunities.

---

14 *Maine Economic Growth Council.*

15 It is important to compare apples to apples and oranges to oranges. As discussed in detail later in this chapter, the Reinventing Maine Government study identified five states with very similar rural/urban populations and geographic distributions; to-wit, Mississippi, Montana, South Dakota, Vermont and Wyoming. In 2001, Mississippi ranked 50th in personal *per capita* income, and it does so today. Montana ranked 44th, and is 36th today. South Dakota was 35th and today it ranks 18th. Vermont was 24th and today it ranks 21st. Wyoming was ranked 15th in terms of personal *per capita* income, and today it ranks 7th.

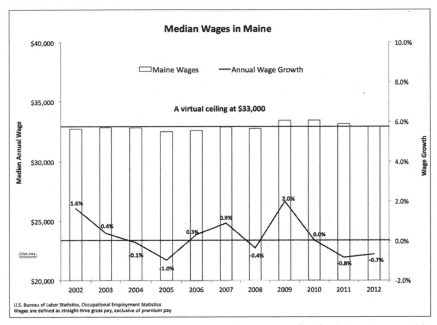

Median Wages in Maine

A virtual ceiling at $33,000

☐ Maine Wages ━ Annual Wage Growth

U.S. Bureau of Labor Statistics, Occupational Employment Statistics
Wages are defined as straight-time gross pay, exclusive of premium pay

Maine's median wages have averaged annual growth of only 0.2% over last decade, less than 1/10 of the average annual inflation rate of 2.4%

Maine wages have averaged about 88% of New England regional wages over the last decade.

In 1990, more than 17,000 Maine workers were employed in the state's paper industry.[16] Today, according to the Maine Pulp and Paper Association, Maine is producing more paper than it ever has, and growing more wood fibre; but only about 7,300 persons are now directly employed in the paper industry, and only three paper companies are among the state's top fifty employers.[17]

When and where they exist, of course, jobs in the paper industry remain excellent jobs, paying an average annual salary of more than $64,800, and the paper industry still contributes more than $470,000,000 annually in payroll to the state's economy.[18] Yet, the average age of a paper worker at Verso's mills, for example, is in the mid-50's and with the forces of productivity and globalization relentlessly pushing down the number of employees required to produce a ton of paper, Maine's young people can't count on explosive job growth in Maine's paper industry.

---

[16] http://boston.com/news/education/higher/articles/2007/07/15/paper_industry_officials_fear_worker_shortage/; U.S. Department of Labor.

[17] Maine Pulp and Paper Association

[18] Id.

In 1960, shoes, textiles and apparel accounted for 30% of all wages paid in Maine, and the total payroll in these industries was even larger than the total payroll in the pulp and paper industry.[20] Today, only New Balance is listed among the state's fifty largest employers. Not a single textile manufacturer or apparel producer appears on the list.[21]

These gut-wrenching changes haven't been confined to what we might call our heritage industries. In 1980, manufacturing jobs generally represented twenty-four percent (24%) of all jobs in Maine. By the mid-2000's, however, less than ten percent (10%) of Maine jobs were in manufacturing.

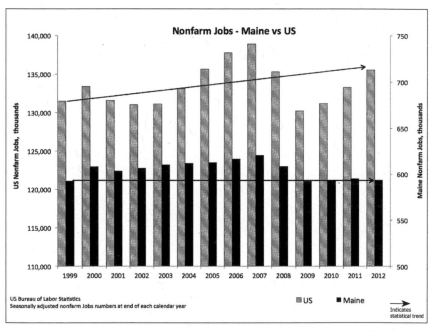

Maine has averaged private sector jobs LOSSES of -0.1% per year over the last decade, while the United States as a whole has averaged 0.3% annual GROWTH.

Maine had fewer non-farm jobs in January, 2013 than in October, 1999, while the rest of the United States added about 4 million non-farm jobs over that same period.

The conclusion, at least with respect to Maine's traditional, heritage industries, is obvious: the jobs of the past are unlikely to be the jobs of the future. Even as we must find

---

[20] "The Maine Economy: Yesterday, Today, and Tomorrow," Prof. Charles S. Colgan, for The Brookings Institution, at p. 6. http://www.growsmartmaine.org/pdfs/maine_economy.pdf

[21] Maine Department of Labor, http://www.maine.gov/labor/cwri/publications/pdf/MaineTop50Employers.pdf

ways for our paper industry – which produces significant payroll, fuels much of our rural economy and makes a huge contribution to the state – to remain competitive, we can no longer count on the industry to employ vastly more Maine workers than it does today. The same is true of other industries that still contribute significantly to state GDP, but do not support the levels of employment that they once did.

Maine's failure to respond to these employment challenges is writ across the Lost Decade. In fact, we had fewer nonfarm jobs in January, 2013 in Maine than we had in October, 1999.

* * *

Demographics, global competition and technology are obvious drivers of the changes we've witnessed and the impacts we've endured, but one major cause of today's opportunity deficit has been our failure during the past ten years to develop long-term goals and objectives and a strategy to achieve them.

Now we find ourselves teetering at the precipice of an increasingly vicious downward cycle, where our past failures to invest and to develop a sound growth strategy continue to drive away both employers and young people – further increasing the economic burden of an aging population, further limiting our governments' tax revenues, and further limiting our communities' abilities to meet our felt obligations.[22]

A vibrant economy, on the other hand, would enhance our quality of life and provide the resources necessary to pursue the policies that Maine people consider important, whether we're talking about the environment, health care, education, public safety or infrastructure improvements.

The challenge we face together in Maine, pure and simple, is how to broaden opportunity by increasing the level of economic activity in our state. Presumably, that's what we all want to achieve, but too often we have taken our eyes off the ball and become bogged down in partisan wrangling over taxes and spending.

---

[22] In coming years, Maine will also face even bigger picture challenges that will be shared by the rest of America. The reversal of what some have called the "demographic dividend" will exert additional pressures. As baby boomers retire, the total number of hours worked on a *per capita* basis will decline, even as more Americans demand public services. A population that is aging, and not replacing its aging citizens with younger, productive workers, faces the prospect of economic stagnation. Further, economists worry about a plateau in educational attainment in this country, coupled with continually escalating costs in higher education (which in turn makes educational attainment that much more difficult), and the continued downward pressure on wages exerted by global manufacturing efficiencies and integrated supply chains. If higher education is priced out of reach, fewer people can acquire the advanced skills and degrees necessary to qualify for higher paying jobs and professional positions in thriving centers of innovation and creativity. If there are more people seeking lower wage, lower skilled jobs – jobs that are at a higher risk of migrating to lower cost environments – the downward pressure on earnings will accelerate even more.

In the 2013 session of the Maine state legislature, for example, arguments over taxes and spending boiled over during the debate over the biennial budget. Yet virtually no time was spent discussing what to do about a healthcare system where costs have spiraled out of control, imposing a big drag on the Maine economy – and a rapidly escalating "tax" on Maine workers.

Taxes and spending are tools – important ones, to be sure, but just tools – that either help us achieve, or get in the way of achieving, the *common* goal of increased economic activity. When we start with blind dogma (e.g., taxes should be higher/lower, or we should spend more/less on public benefits), we are confusing the means with the end; on that path we will never come together on a plan and a strategy. That's one of the reasons why we've been stuck for ten years in Maine – because partisans have been fighting with each other over whose prescription is the best medicine for an economy that we all recognize is in miserable shape.

If instead we will first come together on a vision, there's a far better chance that we can agree on the tools – the plan and the strategy, the right mix of taxes and spending – that we need to employ to reach our goals. As the levels of economic activity increase, we will have more and more flexibility to make choices about taxes and spending.

To create more and better jobs and opportunities for Maine people and to increase our incomes, we need a growth strategy. We need a plan to lower our costs of living and to invest in Maine's future.

2

The North Carolina Example

- The North Carolina example demonstrates that changing a state's direction begins with dialogue, vision and the development of a workable plan. Despite a decade of stagnation and challenges of a magnitude not seen since the Great Depression, there has been no articulation by the State's leaders of an economic development strategy that reflects Maine's new realities.

- Progress is possible when people come together to confront the challenges that face them. The critical factors in North Carolina's transformation were conscious decisions by leaders in the state to invest in their state's competitive advantages and to stick to a long-term plan.

The preceding discussion should raise a host of red flags. This is a crucial time in Maine's history. Our economy is small and our incomes are limited. Our expenses are high in both relative terms and in absolute dollars. The development of a strategy – a coherent plan based upon clearly articulated goals and objectives – has to be the starting point for moving Maine forward. Indeed, in large part it has been the absence of a plan that has impeded Maine's progress for the past decade.

If our elected policymakers – our governor and legislators – fail to develop the strategy for success that Maine needs, no one will.

In today's conflict-driven political environment, of course, the idea of bringing people, communities and policymakers together to tackle the challenges we face may seem almost far-fetched. Yet this is exactly what is required. We need to develop goals, objectives, and strategies to achieve them in which our neighbors and we are all "invested" and to which our state and local governments have subscribed.

Hard working Mainers deserve a plan and a strategy, based upon a shared vision and shared goals, that will bring economic opportunity to all corners of our state.

Other states have done it. So can Maine.

Some states literally have transformed themselves through the development and application of smart, long-term strategies that have taken advantage of their strengths. Those states have invested in their competitive advantages and have reaped the positive results that a solid and substantive plan can have on economic opportunity and prosperity.

North Carolina is a good example of economic development planning that has worked.[23]

Like Maine several decades before, North Carolina in the 1950's and early 1960's was an economy in transition from a state in which agriculture played a major role to one in which manufacturing – especially furniture and textiles – began to dominate.

Textile mills and furniture factories flourished in the lower-wage, lower-cost environment of the state's Piedmont region. Much of North Carolina's manufacturing job growth came at the expense of Maine and other northeast states where the mills and factories of the nineteenth and early twentieth centuries had supported generations of workers.

During this time North Carolina's economic development strategy focused principally and simply on providing transportation infrastructure (generally roads) and easy access to low-cost labor. Manufacturing employment grew from roughly 20% of the state's total employment in 1900 to nearly 33% by 1960.

The low cost manufacturing economy model was creating jobs, but the jobs did not pay well. Even as manufacturing employment grew, and in fact grew faster than manufacturing employment in the rest of the country, wages continued to lag the national average. In 1960 North Carolina's *per capita* income was just 71% of United States *per capita* income.

The critical factor in North Carolina's subsequent transformation was that the political, business, and academic leaders in the state recognized the limitations of a low-cost, low-wage model *and acted on it*; they made a conscious decision to develop higher skill, higher wage jobs in industries that depended on more advanced technologies.

By the end of the 20th century, the state's economy had been transformed from one dominated by textiles, furniture and tobacco to one in which technology, pharmaceuticals, banking, food processing and vehicle parts became the industrial leaders.

---

[23] *See*, in connection with the ensuing discussion, "*An Overview of Economic Development Policy in North Carolina: Transforming the State from Poverty to Prosperity*," (2010) R. Carlisle, former Secretary, N.C. Department of Commerce.

North Carolina's *per capita* income soared in comparison with the rest of America, from 71% of the average United States *per capita* income in 1960 to 91.48% of the U.S. average in 1999.[24] A plan can make a difference.

How did the state accomplish this dramatic transformation? How did the economic fortunes of North Carolina's workers improve so markedly? What are the lessons that we in Maine can learn from what they did? Just as important, what are the lessons that we should *not* learn?

Lesson number one? It wasn't an accident.

North Carolina became a technology leader, created economic opportunity, and raised incomes and living standards because political and government leaders acted in partnership with business and academia to develop a plan that eventually would change the economic landscape of the state. North Carolina's leaders focused on three policies to guide its plan for economic transformation: economic development, workforce development and lessening inequities.

Government and business leaders and officials from research universities in Raleigh, Durham and Chapel Hill first met in 1956 to formulate a policy response to a disturbing trend in the region's workforce: the out-migration of educated graduates from these universities to other states. They determined that an important response would be to build upon the strengths and reputations of the universities, and then, as part of a broad effort to diversify the industrial base, to package and market a regional resource of knowledge workers to potential employers.

Lower-wage workers were available in abundance, but in order to keep more educated, skilled workers in the state, it was essential to attract employers in a position to hire them.

Thus was born the concept of a creating a premier research complex that would soon be known as The North Carolina Research Triangle. Governor Terry Sanford continued the effort begun by leaders in the late 1950's and recruited the first major investments in the Research Triangle, the National Institute for Environmental Health and IBM in 1965.

Today, Research Triangle Park is comprised of fifty research and development companies and organizations employing 32,000 workers.

---

[24] http://www.ncosc.net/financial/05_cafr/T11.pdf

Building and promoting a research complex wasn't in itself what led to the dramatic changes in North Carolina's economy. What accomplished these changes was a series of integrated steps – rational, planned, sustained steps – that, taken together, positioned the state and its citizens for better economic opportunities and higher incomes. These steps included workforce development centers that provided training for jobs demanded by growing industries and employers (information technology and biotechnology); entrepreneurship training; and the seeding of a venture capital industry.

North Carolina established a Microelectronics Center, a Biotechnology Center, the North Carolina High School of Science and Mathematics, and small business and technology centers. These centers provided infrastructure for growing industries, workforce training, networking, and early stage funding for companies with high growth potential.

North Carolina also made aggressive use of economic development incentives to attract employers, including cash and generous tax incentives. In the late 1990's, North Carolina created tax credits for job creation, acquisition of equipment, workforce training and research and development.

North Carolina became a poster child for economic transformation, and Research Triangle Park remains an oft-cited example of big-picture economic development thinking that works. Today, North Carolina's economy is far more diverse, far more vibrant and far more durable than was the case before its leaders sat down a half-century ago and said, "This thing is broken, and we have to fix it."

* * *

North Carolina is not a paradigm for Maine. It's experience is not one we should try to precisely replicate. Nonetheless, there are two important aspects of the North Carolina that deserve our attention.

First, the same industries that left Maine *later* left North Carolina; North Carolina consciously and strategically retooled, but we still haven't.

Second, the North Carolina experience illustrates how elected officials can inspire and lead the kind of long-range thinking, planning and investment that harnesses the energies and imagination of business, labor, academia and government to accomplish change and development that make a lasting difference in the economic opportunities and incomes of citizens.

Leaders in North Carolina saw the writing on the wall. They knew that competing for lower-wage jobs in manufacturing was not sustainable in a global manufacturing environment that facilitated outsourcing to lower-cost production sites. They acknowledged the global trends and argued for paradigm shifts in strategy and focus. The results have been dramatic.[25]

On the other hand, it became clear more than decades ago that fewer employees would be needed to harvest the timber, produce the paper, process the seafood and otherwise generate equivalent economic output in Maine's traditional industries. Yet even as the country and Maine in recent years have confronted exceptional economic challenges not seen since the Great Depression, since 2002 there has been no articulation at the state level of an economic development strategy, vision or plan that reflects Maine's new realities.

[25] North Carolina isn't perfect. It has high levels of unemployment in down economic cycles, and, in fact, its 2011 *per capita* income of $36,028 trails Maine's *per capita* income of $38,299. However, costs of living are considerably lower than In Maine, and North Carolina's tax base is much broader. More to the point, North Carolina's progress from its earlier, much lower base is something Maine should envy.

3
The Lesson of The Lost Decade:
Maine Needs a Vision and a Plan

• Maine is right back where we were a decade ago. Employment, median wages and incomes are virtually unchanged through six legislatures and three terms of two governors from two different parties.

• A growing economy doesn't happen by accident. Our greatest failing has been the failure of our state's leaders to craft a plan for Maine – all of Maine.

• The right tests of good governance: Are Maine citizens better off? Do our kids have a future in Maine? Is Maine a place of opportunity?

• Maine can be the economic turnaround story of **this** generation.

The numbers and statistics recounted in Chapter 1 tell a profoundly tragic story: *Maine's economy has stood still for more than a decade.*

As our economy has continued to evolve from one with a solid base of manufacturing to one dominated by the provision of services, employment has continued to shrink through six legislatures and three terms of two different governors.

That failure to protect and create opportunity in Maine has exacted a massive toll on the day-to-day lives of thousands of Maine people, shrinking their hopes, dreams and aspirations. Thousands of Maine's young people have fled our state, intensifying a vicious demographic cycle where Maine's population – already the oldest in America – is also aging faster than any other state's.

Why has Maine struggled so over the Lost Decade?

Is it, as *Forbes* has suggested, because of high taxes and a business climate less welcoming than what can be found in other states? Is it crippling energy and health care costs? Is it our crumbling infrastructure? Low rates of investment? An aging workforce whose skills don't match the needs of employers? Maine's largely unavoidable circumstances – our location, geography, and population distribution?

In fact, these are probably all right answers. But they are not *all* of the right answers. Most importantly, they don't include the most important answer of all – the answer most within our control to change.

The fact is that our greatest failing – for ten long years – has been the failure of our state's leaders to craft a plan for Maine and to implement it; we have failed to invest in a long-term statewide strategy to stabilize Maine's economic position, leverage Maine's competitive advantages and position Maine people for greater opportunity and prosperity. Nothing we have done has been tied to a coherent vision and a larger plan, and the bitter harvest of that failure is the economic growth that we have not seen, the jobs and incomes that we do not have.

We do face exceptional challenges in Maine – challenges of geography, location, demographics and more – but they are neither immutable nor insurmountable, and they need not be permanent. These challenges cry out for a plan and the shared determination to overcome them, and it is the absence of a plan and leadership that has left us spinning our wheels in a decade-long rut.

Clearly, the policies and programs of the past decade – whether advanced from the left or the right – have failed to move the needle.

All the budget cuts the most hard-hearted among us might imagine and all of the bureaucratic reforms that the most efficient among us might prescribe haven't made our economy any larger – and by themselves won't.

All of the well-funded public assistance programs the most generous among us might suggest and all of the regulations that the most cautious among us might propose haven't properly positioned Mainers to compete in the global economy – and by themselves won't.

If we can't get our health care costs under control, we won't be in a position to leverage our competitive advantages.

If we don't repair our systems of public education, our children's opportunities here in Maine won't be any brighter.

If we don't make investments in roads and bridges and rail and in bringing young people to live and work here, Maine will not have the human and capital infrastructure that a growing and vibrant economy requires.

The lesson of the Lost Decade is clear: Maine needs to approach economic growth in a different way. We need to make and follow a positive, affirmative plan that will transform Maine's economy and create meaningful opportunity for Maine people.

The plans and strategies in the chapters that follow can help Maine become healthier, smarter, stronger, younger, and more prosperous. These plans and strategies are starting points for a conversation that all of us who love Maine need to have about our state's future.

All around our state, often in unexpected places, there is evidence of the rewards that can be won with planning, collaboration, and investment. Not long ago the Downeast community of Eastport was a town that most thought had seen its best days pass by years ago. Yet, it is once again a thriving seaport, and on a cold Monday evening in January 2013 there were five restaurants open for dinner... and only one vacant storefront on Sea Street.

Eastport today is a hotbed of economic growth that was jumpstarted by community leaders who came together just as leaders came together years ago in North Carolina, focused their collective attention on Eastport's competitive advantages, made a plan, invested in it and stayed the course.

Our years of economic stagnation – Maine's Lost Decade – should teach us that wildly shifting policies and plugging holes as leaks appear are no way to build an economy.

Maine has swung from one "strategy" to another since 2003. For eight long years we overspent and over-regulated; then we turned to an aggressive and nearly exclusive focus on the expense side of the state's ledger—one that often has been patently unfair, to boot.

Both strategies – if you can call them that – have failed to bring Maine lasting growth and more jobs. Our incomes aren't as high as they should be; our economy isn't stronger; and our prospects for future growth aren't any better.

Both strategies have failed the tests of good governance.

The right tests for good governance aren't based on party dogma or partisan rants. The right tests aren't whether state government is taxing and spending more or less, or if it is imposing more or fewer rules and regulations. The right tests of good governance are performance and outcomes: Are Maine citizens' better off? Do our kids have a future in Maine? Is Maine a place of opportunity?

Opportunity must be our overarching goal for Maine. As a community we don't owe a guarantee of success to anyone, but we do owe to our children – to anyone who chooses to live in this great state – an opportunity to grow, to learn, to compete, to prosper and to succeed. In any enterprise, public or private, we can achieve great success when we remove obstacles and make opportunities available for every one of us to achieve his or her greatest potential as a human being.

I deeply believe that opportunity can make magic. It can make miracles happen. It can spell the difference between an entire state's success or failure. Opportunity is a rocket fuel that can propel an economy to new heights. If broad opportunity becomes part and parcel of the Maine way of life, we will keep our children here and attract talented people to live here with us, creating jobs and economic growth.

We need to stop talking about "more government" versus "less government." We need to stop debating the relative merits of two failed strategies. We need to follow Eastport's example of an unremitting focus on creating opportunity – removing barriers and making public investments in common assets.

When we talk about the role of our state government, we need to focus on problem solving instead of problem causing, on smart instead of foolish, on active instead of reactive, on innovative rather than conventional, on foresight versus no-sight, and on collaboration instead of confrontation.

A dogmatic, tired, partisan agenda won't cut it any more. That kind of agenda is a poor substitute for a vision, a plan and a strategy. That kind of agenda won't get the job done; it won't promote jobs and economic growth, reform our tax structure, and control the costs and improve the quality of education and health care.

Let's together figure out the answer to the questions that are important to our futures and our kids' futures: How can Maine people excel and prosper in a worldwide economic environment that values distinction, excellence and creativity; that relentlessly seeks a younger and better educated workforce; and that wants and needs sustainable, traceable healthy products whose quality can be trusted and whose brand is known?

A growing economy doesn't happen by accident. It happens, as it did in North Carolina and in Eastport, when leaders describe a vision of the future that engages broad support; when they identify the goals and objectives that can make the vision real; and when they fashion a strategy for meeting those goals that makes good sense, that is even-handed and fair, and that motivates a shared commitment to gain shared rewards.

Successful businesses do this every day. So do families making budgets, mortgage payments and investing savings for college or retirement.

The same kinds of opportunities that Eastport protected and created exist across the State of Maine. We just need to form and articulate together an economic development strategy that reflects an understanding of Maine's competitive advantages and sets a course to leverage them into success.

If Mainers believe in a common vision of our state's future, believe that the goals are sound, and believe that the plan is fair and has a good chance of working, we will be able to sustain a long-term and shared commitment to see it through.

No one person has the "right" vision. We need to draw from all of us the elements of a common vision for Maine with which most of us are more or less comfortable and in which we all have confidence. We need to create and embrace a common vision of where Maine should be in 20 or 30 years and undertake a shared commitment to a plan that will get us there.

As North Carolina was in an earlier time, Maine can be the economic turnaround story of this generation. It will take vision and imagination, tough and courageous decisions, broadly shared commitment to a plan that we all understand, and a sustained, committed and collaborative effort to make it work.

Opportunity will beget prosperity if we focus on becoming healthier, smarter, stronger and younger. Fashioning an investment strategy and a plan to help make that happen is the subject of Part Two.

Part Two:

A Great Place To Live...
and To Make A Living

4
Healthier, Smarter, Stronger and Younger

- Maine can be a good place to live and a place to make a good living.

- The choices we make and the policies we pursue can dramatically increase opportunity for Mainers if we confront our most serious challenges head on.

- Let's set some ambitious goals for 2020: the healthiest state in the nation; educational proficiency; double the visitors; twice the agricultural land; and more births than deaths.

As we make a plan and invest in our children's futures, Maine will see new jobs and vibrant economic growth. The opportunities that we protect and begin to create in a newly growing economy will spawn even more opportunities, and we will replace the vicious cycle of the Lost Decade with a new and virtuous cycle.

With opportunity as our touchstone, Maine will be both a good place to live and a place to make a good living. Here are the broad outlines that we'll discuss in greater detail below.

Healthier

By many measures, Maine is a healthy state; the United Health Foundation ranked us 9th out of 50 states in its 2012 report. But health care in Maine costs insurers, patients and taxpayers too much and is inaccessible for too many of us. On both of those counts – cost and access – we've been moving in the wrong directions.

A plan for Maine should eliminate those barriers and make good health care available to all Maine citizens at a reasonable cost.

Smarter

American companies are hiring fewer and fewer people. Productivity in manufacturing is way up, but employment isn't; that's certainly the case in Maine's paper industry, where we're producing more paper with fewer and fewer employees.

As with health care, we're not raising, spending or investing our public education dollars wisely enough; we've not organized our education efforts as well as we should; and we're not educating, training and retaining the kind of workforce that employers increasingly require.

A plan for Maine should strengthen our schools, empower good teachers and principals, and better prepare our children.

Stronger

Successful businesses pay attention to what they do well; Apple doesn't make toasters or boats. World-class athletes seldom try to compete in sports or events where they have limited skills; Michael Jordan failed at baseball.

The same goes for states. Maine's competitive advantages – those characteristics that *do* make us different and *can* make us stronger – aren't hard to spot. Lurking in our location, our natural resources and our people and communities is vast untapped potential for economic growth.

A plan for Maine should turn that huge potential into real opportunity by investing in our backbone infrastructure of roads, bridges, railroads and ports; by reforming our tax structure so that we create the means to make investments in smart and fair ways; and by building the Maine brand.

Government has an important role to play in making Maine stronger, but the road to rational government decision-making is considerably rockier when the ways in which we elect our leaders are out of synch with our politics and our values. When rational and responsible debate about competing ideas is overwhelmed by money and negative advertising, democracy is weakened and governing suffers.

A plan for Maine should strengthen our political processes so that we will make investment decisions that are the product of a healthy democracy.

Younger

The greatest obstacle to Maine's prosperity isn't our climate, our location or our taxes. Rather, it's the age of our population. The most important imperative of all – the central element in this vision of Maine's future – is that Maine *must* get younger, fast. All of our plans for prosperity, for a growing and vibrant economy, depend on this element of our strategy.

A plan for Maine should employ every innovative and cost-effective tool that we can invent or borrow to make Maine younger.

Bicentennial Goals

During World War II, 30,000 workers at the yards of the New England Shipbuilding Corporation in South Portland built 266 Liberty Ships over a period of four and a half years. The S.S. *Jeremiah O'Brien* – now a monument – was built in the South Portland yard in just 56 days.

Those Maine workers had goals to meet. They met those goals because they understood the importance of what they were doing for themselves and for their children. They were inspired to work together and to succeed.

We need to rekindle in Maine the same can-do spirit of optimism and collaboration. Let's start by setting some bicentennial goals – challenges that we will meet by Maine's 200th birthday in 2020.

- Maine will match the national growth rate in jobs and employment, double our growth rate from the 2002-2012 decade in *per capita* GDP and quadruple our average annual growth in median wages.

- Maine will be the healthiest state in America while Mainers will spend less on healthcare than we do today. Every Mainer will have access to preventive healthcare, and no Mainer will face the risk of financial ruin brought on by the costs of care.

- Every child in Maine will read proficiently by the end of third grade, and financial circumstances no longer will bar a student from post-high school training or education.

- The number of annual visitors to Maine will be twice the number who visited in 2012, and each of them will spend 50% more on meals, lodging sightseeing and recreation. Maine's will be a four-season tourism economy.

- The amount of agricultural land in Maine will be twice the 1.3 million acres in 2012, and the acreage in year-round cultivation will increase by twenty-fold.

- The number of births in Maine will outstrip the number of deaths, and Maine will be getting younger faster than many other states.

These are ambitious goals – but they sure beat no goals at all.

Our natural resources, our communities and our people can make Maine an economic powerhouse, if we provide strength of will and a purpose. All we need is a vision that most of us share, a plan and a strategy that most of us believe in, and goals that most of us embrace.

5

Healthier:
Better Healthcare at Lower Cost

- Reforming the way we manage health care challenges can save money and improve our quality of life.

- We need to apply traditional Maine concepts of value and innovation to our healthcare system. Rather than fighting the new federal health care law, Maine should be actively managing its implementation in a way that works best for Maine.

- Providing access to essential health care for every Maine citizen and rewarding healthy behaviors will make Maine more competitive as a place to live and work.

We are spending more for health care in Maine without getting the value we want and need. Too many of us don't have access to quality health care, and all of us are paying too much. In order to create opportunity in Maine, we need to get health care and education (next chapter) right. The costs and inefficiencies in both systems are the biggest barriers to growing Maine's economy.

Maine's high health care costs rank us near the top.

- Maine had the 5th highest health care spending *per capita* in 2009, at $9,123 in 2012 dollars, 25% higher than the national average

- More than 20 cents of every dollar each of us spends in Maine goes to health care.

- Maine's health care spending more than tripled from 1993 to 2009, accelerating faster than in most other states.

- Maine's health care expenditures are growing two to three times faster than spending on other goods and services.

None of this is good news.

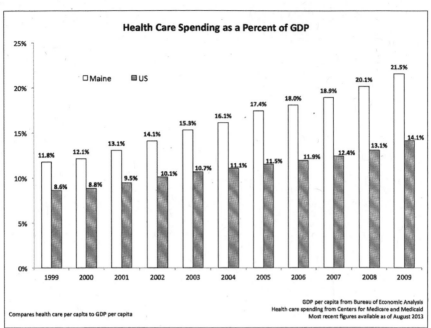

Health Care Spending as a Percent of GDP

Compares health care per capita to GDP per capita

GDP per capita from Bureau of Economic Analysis
Health care spending from Centers for Medicare and Medicaid
Most recent figures available as of August 2013

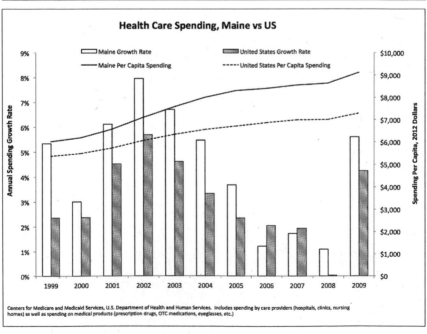

Health Care Spending, Maine vs US

Centers for Medicare and Medicaid Services, U.S. Department of Health and Human Services. Includes spending by care providers (hospitals, clinics, nursing homes) as well as spending on medical products (prescription drugs, OTC medications, eyeglasses, etc.)

- The health care spending delta between Maine and the US has gone from 3.2% of GDP in 1999 to 7.4% in 2009, increasing by nearly two and a half times in a decade.

- Maine has increased spending on health care as a percent of GDP by 83% over ten years.

- Average annual health care spending growth as a percent of GDP in Maine is 6.3% per year versus 5.1% for the US.

- In 2012, Mainers spent on average $1,827 more per person on health care than the average U.S. citizen, up from just $652 more in 1999, and that difference has been growing every year.

- Maine has averaged 4.4% health care spending growth per annum from 1999-2009 versus 3.0% for the U.S. as a whole.[26]

We know that the lion's share of avoidable costs in Maine's health care system can be traced to excessive equipment and facilities driving unnecessary procedures and costs; to costs imposed by a claims-based system of insurance coverage and reimbursement; to weak incentives that fail to encourage healthy behaviors; and to the failure to provide primary and secondary preventive care to all Maine citizens. And we've known all this for years.[27]

We all share the angst about these trends, and we all want to spend less and get more value. Yet, against a background of high costs, excessive spending and diminished access, in recent years Maine has been taking too many steps that are making our problems bigger and our circumstances worse. For example...

- We have no statewide health care plan or budget and state oversight of health care systems spending is too limited. Maine's hospitals and other providers now can spend twice as much on equipment and three times as much on facilities before state approval is required, reinforcing incentives to order expensive procedures and further escalating costs throughout the Maine health care system.

---

[26] http://bangordailynews.com/2013/04/26/opinion/why-is-maine-5th-in-us-for-health-care-spending/; http://www.cm.gov/Research-Statistics-Data-and-Systems/Statistics-Trends-and-Reports/NationalHealthExpendData/NationalHealthAccounts StateHealthAccountsResidence.html. Most recent figures available as of August, 2013.

[27] The 2008 report of Maine's Advisory Council on Health System Development reported that there are four reasons why Maine's costs are high: excessive use of emergency rooms, too many duplicative hospital facilities, high levels of chronic illness and an older population.

- Insurance companies in Maine are now permitted to charge more for less, while receiving a $22 million subsidy from taxpayers in the bargain. Plus, insurers in Maine can now raise their premiums by as much as 10% a year without the permission of the State of Maine Insurance Commission.

- Because Maine has "opted out" of Medicaid expansion under the Affordable Care Act and is booting off the MaineCare rolls many who are currently covered, tens of thousands of Mainers will be without access to preventive health care of any kind, and without access to quality healthcare when they become ill, except in the emergency rooms of Maine hospitals. This will drive costs higher and opportunities lower.

The problems we face with access to quality health care in Maine – and the excessive costs we pay for it – aren't caused by federal policies and won't be fixed by the Affordable Care Act ("ACA" or "Obamacare"). The problems are largely of our own making right here in Maine.

Maine's health care system for the most part has been permitted to design itself, even though taxpayers are footing the bill. The health care system in too many ways ends up serving narrow institutional interests instead of primarily serving the broader public interest. That needs to change if we want to create opportunity and see Maine's economy grow. Maine needs to develop and follow a statewide strategy that applies traditional Maine concepts of value and innovation to our healthcare system.

We can make Maine more competitive as a place to live and to work by achieving a healthier population and workforce at a lower and more sustainable cost. Today the system is broken, but it can be fixed. Some of the principles that ought to guide a better approach include these:

- In a state that values opportunity and growth, universal access to quality health care is centrally important. *Every* Mainer should have a "medical home" and a primary care provider.

- Maine's entire health care system should reward high quality care and positive health outcomes – not high volumes of procedures – provided by physicians, hospitals and other health care professionals.

- Maine's health care infrastructure should be designed to provide the services Maine people need at costs they can afford: clinics and emergency and ambulatory care centers in community service centers with telemedicine links to major medical centers; ambulances and helicopters to transport patients who urgently need higher level care; high-functioning, critical care hospitals in sensible locations.

- Quality should be improved and costs reduced by emphasizing both primary preventive care (because it can lower the incidence of many acute and chronic diseases and accidents) and secondary preventive care (because it can reduce the complications of unavoidable chronic illness).

- Reformed incentives should cause patients and providers alike to be accountable for their own roles and behaviors. All of us should have "skin in the game," to share responsibility for good health care outcomes.

- Maine should promote initiatives to improve population health and physical and mental fitness, and should have a more robust public health effort to help assure a safe and healthy environment and to help prepare for disasters.

The key to implementing these important principles is having a smart statewide strategy and the right organizational structures in place.

Today in Maine most large employers (including hospitals themselves) have bypassed the conventional health insurance offerings from Anthem and others because they can obtain more value for their employees at lower costs through self-insurance, rewards for good behaviors and an emphasis on preventive care. That's good for them and good for Mainers who happen to be employed by these large employers; but most Mainers aren't.

Too many Mainers today either are uninsured and dependent on expensive emergency room care, or they are dependent on expensive individual and small group plans where health insurers and providers recover the costs (and more) of providing care to the uninsured. This is driving our costs higher, isn't working for anyone – and it's unfair.

Regardless of where we sit on the political spectrum, most of us in Maine believe that *fairness* is particularly important when it comes to health care. A friend who happens to be a politically active Republican wrote this message in an email exchange during the 2013 tussle over MaineCare expansion and the question of whether Maine should fight with the federal government:

"One answer from the extreme right is to let poor people remain at risk because it's not government's business, it's the only answer our nation can afford and some among the poor have brought it on themselves.

People on the left are often obsessed with expanding government sponsored care without paying much attention to who deserves it, how well it works or how much it costs.

People earnestly engaged in a discussion of health policy should accept as axiomatic:

1. *That civil society must respond to the parable of the Good Samaritan and its moral analogs;*

2. *That the American medical system is unacceptably expensive, wasteful and inefficient; and*

3. *That opportunities for state sponsored improvements to population health go well beyond the question of how to deliver medical care."*

In an irresponsible fit of partisanship, Maine has now turned its back on hundreds of millions of dollars of federal funds that would have been made available to plan a new health care exchange in Maine and to provide health care to thousands of Maine citizens. The result is that Maine taxpayers are paying for better health care access for citizens in other states while our own state officials refuse to accept the same benefits for Maine.

Rather than fighting implementation of the new ACA at every turn, Maine state government should be actively managing its implementation so that it works best for Maine. Most importantly, Maine should take full advantage of the opportunities for innovation enabled by the ACA through the creation of Accountable Care Organizations (ACO's) and by correcting deficiencies in existing state programs.

• Doctors and hospitals in ACO's work directly with purchasers to provide best-practice health services, with greater accountability and at lower costs. ACO providers accept responsibility on a contractual basis to make a negotiated set of health care services available to a defined group of patients.

• Working with state employee organizations and other public agencies that provide health benefits, the State of Maine can support the development of ACO's as alternatives to conventional health insurance by leveraging its considerable purchasing power in the health care marketplace.

- Instead of letting the federal government impose a one-size-fits-all scheme on us, Maine should create a Maine Health Exchange under the ACA and offer new ACO arrangements as another coverage option for small businesses and individuals purchasing their coverage through the Maine-specific Health Exchange.

Whether they are old or young, employed or unemployed, whoever they are and wherever they live, all Mainers are entitled to essential health care – first because it is the right, fair and morally responsible thing to do, and second because it is the financially and economically smart thing to do. We need to make certain that the care is appropriate and not excessive, because that is the fiscally responsible thing to do. The reforms described here should make it possible to do both.

Maine has a huge opportunity – to stay in the very top tier of America's healthiest places to live and to work while at the same time muscling down our heath care costs. By effecting major reform in our health care systems, we can provide access to essential health care for every Maine citizen, reward healthy behaviors and best health care practices and make Maine more competitive as a place to live and to work.

Reducing health care costs and improving access is a central part of our plan for Maine. Achieving a healthier population and workforce at a lower and more sustainable cost will be one of the best investments we make in Maine's future.

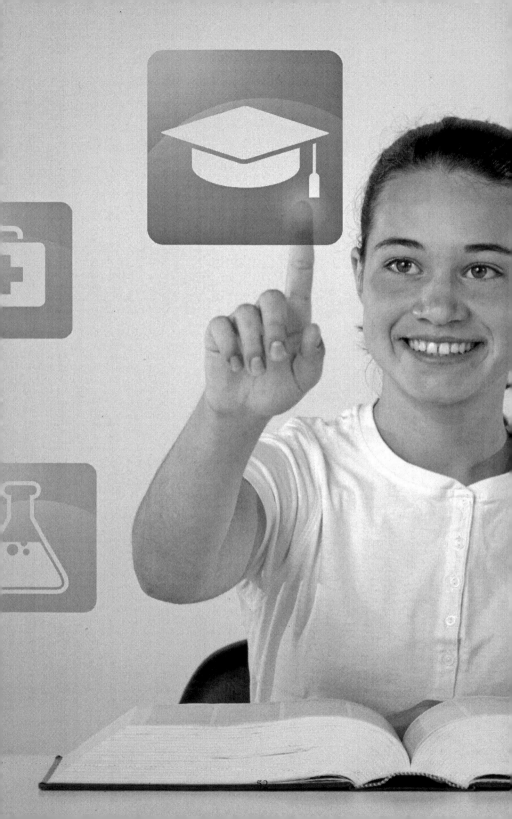

6

Smarter Investments:
Making Maine Stronger

- The states in America with the best education systems often have the strongest economies.

- Maine's costs per pupil are considerably higher than the national average. We should insist on reforms designed around the needs of students, their families and their communities.

- We should re-examine the way we fund public education in Maine.

- We should extend the school year and shine a spotlight on teacher success.

- The costs of post-secondary education in Maine are too high and the success rates are too low. One governing body and central administration for our community colleges and four-year university campuses would mean closer collaboration, better allocation of precious resources and greater efficiency.

The most important thing to know about education is this: as machines get smarter and people don't, American companies are hiring fewer and fewer people. Productivity in manufacturing is way up, but employment isn't. (Both corporate profits and unemployment have been at record levels because employers are reinvesting profits where it makes the most sense in terms of productivity and profits – that is, in machines instead of people.)

Maine's manufacturing GDP, for example was about the same in 2011 as it was in 2000, but two big changes occurred in the Maine manufacturing employment base: First, the number of jobs in Maine manufacturing fell during that same period by 37%, so 30,000 or so Mainers whose skills were once needed to produce about $5 billion worth of paper and other goods aren't needed by their employers any more. Second, the education and skills training needed in our workforce have increased dramatically.

Maine is not the only state to face the challenges of higher productivity. All of America is now lagging behind the rest of the world in educating our children for jobs in the knowledge economy. But Maine has been among the slowest states to do anything about it where we could do the most good – in education. We are beset with problems of organization, cost and allocation of resources.

Moreover, as in the case of health care, Maine's costs per pupil are considerably higher than the national average, despite *per capita* income in Maine being well below the national average. Adjusted for regional cost differences for salaries, Maine in 2010 had the sixth highest per pupil expenditure rate in the nation, almost perfectly mirroring our health care cost ranking. And although Maine's K-12 enrollments declined precipitously during the last decade – hitting rural areas of our state particularly hard – school expenses continued to rise.

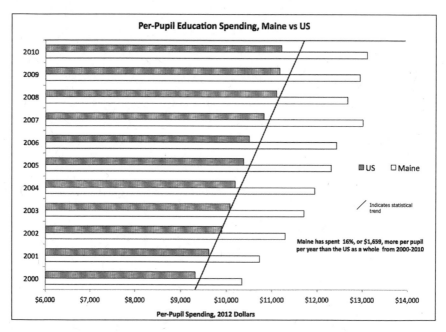

Expenditures include instruction, instruction-related, support services, and other elementary/secondary current expenditures, but exclude expenditures on capital outlay, other programs, and interest on long-term debt. U.S. Department of Education, National Center for Education Statistics, Common Core of Data. Most recent statistics available as of August, 2013.

Maine has spent 16%, or $1,659, more per pupil per year than the US as a whole from 2000-2010.

Despite our rising costs, however, good teachers in Maine are not as well paid as they should be. Maine ranks 39th in the nation in average teachers' salaries, and we rank last among the New England states.

It's time to take a fresh look at education, to get smarter about how we use our resources, and to insist on innovation and reform designed around the needs of students, their families and their communities.

Here are some ways that we can begin to do that...

1. Accelerate Early Childhood Education

In order for Maine to achieve our desired outcomes for children – high school graduation and college degrees or occupational certificates that prepare them for jobs in the new economy – we must start by improving and expanding early childhood education.

All children in Maine should receive, at a minimum, appropriate developmental screening and assistance so that they enter kindergarten or pre-kindergarten with the necessary social-emotional, cognitive and early language and literacy skills that prepare them for success in school. As we free up resources to invest or reinvest in education, one of our top priorities must be achieving universal access to high quality early care and education across the entire state.

School readiness and academic success starts with early childhood education. Evidence consistently points to early childhood experiences having lasting impacts on later success in life. As a child's brain grows, the nature and quality of early experience establishes either a sturdy or a fragile foundation for all of the development that follows. Getting things right the first time is easier—and much less expensive—than trying to fix things later.

2. Provide Greater Rewards for Better Teaching and More Innovation

One thing we know for certain about high quality education is that the single most important ingredient is the quality of the teaching.

Many aspects of our current systems for teacher compensation don't serve either our children or the public well. Good, effective teachers don't get paid enough, and the system doesn't sufficiently incentivize teacher collaboration and effective professional mentoring. We need to shine a spotlight on teacher success, reward it, learn from it and replicate it.

Educators and teams of educators who demonstrate their ability to improve student achievement should be rewarded for their success. The current teacher compensation system in most school districts in Maine is a simplistic, seniority-based system that doesn't treat teaching as a profession, making no distinction between those who lead and teach effectively and those who do not. Moreover, together with starting salaries that are often too low, it is a system that likely discourages the best teachers from staying in the profession or from coming to Maine in the first place.

Teachers and principals can help establish reliable methods of measuring student growth and assessing how much a student has improved over the course of a year. We should use those measures, along with reliable test scores, as key building blocks, not simply incidental measures, in rebuilding teacher compensation systems so that they reward educators, teams and schools that have accelerated student progress. Rewards should not be limited to higher pay. Teachers and other professional educators can design new and more effective ways to reward successful collaboration, improve working conditions and to support opportunities for school leadership and professional development.

As we provide more incentives and rewards for the best teaching, we also need to provide similar incentives and rewards for innovation that accelerates and deepens student learning. I remain a strong proponent of charter public schools and additional statewide magnet schools – for marine sciences, the creative arts and foreign languages. One of the reasons I support those alternatives is that they introduce important innovation into public education. The fact is, though, that there will be relatively few charter and magnet schools in Maine; by far the greatest number of our students will be educated in public schools in Maine's 164 school districts. And so we need to work hard at innovating in our regular public schools, too. As the Casco Bay High School in Portland and other innovative schools have demonstrated, it can be done. The state ought to provide incentives in that direction, and then encourage all Maine schools to replicate the successes and reward those that do.

3. Increase Time in School

At 175 days, Maine currently has one of the shortest school calendars in the nation, five fewer than the national average. Our students can't catch up and surpass their counterparts in other states with an abbreviated calendar. The short school calendar deprives teachers of both the time for instruction and for professional development they need to help our students get to the top. We should extend the academic calendar in Maine by a total of ten days, and we should at the very least think about scheduling the school year in ways that better match our school calendars with summer job opportunities across the state.

4. Preserve Community Schools... To Help Preserve Communities

Few issues in recent years have proven more divisive and contentious in Maine than the issue of school district consolidation. Ordering consolidation according to an ill-advised and short-sighted set of criteria was one of the biggest public policy mistakes that Maine has made in generations.

Rather than penalize chiefly rural communities for failing to consolidate school districts, we should create incentives for schools and districts in both rural and urban regions of the state to re-design themselves in cost effective ways, in some cases with broader community purposes, so that they can improve educational opportunities for their children while continuing to play a central role in community life.

In many of our rural communities, consolidation was viewed as a death warrant for the local community school – and often for the town itself. Residents in many small Maine communities believe that the survival of their local school is necessary for their community's well-being and very survival. Because our rural communities are part and parcel of Maine's attraction to visitors and to prospective new residents, those communities are one of Maine's important competitive advantages; their survival is important to all Mainers, regardless of where we live.

On the other hand, the fact remains that declining enrollments in rural areas and the duplication of facilities and administration in both rural and urban areas have combined to drive per pupil expenditures across the state to excessive levels. It's clear we need to look for solutions.

We can make serious gains in both efficiency and effectiveness in school districts across the state – not only in our rural communities, but also in large urban areas like greater Portland – if we encourage local leadership to identify opportunities and implement them, and if the state then rewards such instances of local initiative.

In some cases, local officials may decide that consolidation is the best available alternative, both in economic and educational terms, but that needn't mean that valuable public assets go unused. Schools closed as a consequence of declining enrollments could become part of a network of community service centers offering early childhood programs, parenting classes, vocational and non-traditional academic offerings and health care, all focused on improving educational and health outcomes and preserving communities.

5. Fix School Funding to Create Opportunity for All Maine Kids

Public charter schools are an important addition to our state's education options, and they hold out the prospect of demonstrating the value of new structures, methods and curricula for all of Maine. Because there is an appropriately rigorous system in place for considering and approving new charter schools, however, they will be established in only a small minority of Maine's school districts.

Should the per-pupil costs of educating children in these schools be borne only by the districts from whence they come, even if the migration of a small number of students to charter schools doesn't – can't – change the overall costs of education in those communities?

Of course not. Yet, that very controversy – over the appropriate source of funding for Maine's new public charter schools – erupted in the winter of 2013, becoming the latest chapter in the history of a school funding structure in Maine that isn't understood, isn't entirely fair, and isn't working.

When the legislature enacted LD 1 in 2004, the State of Maine made a commitment to fund 55% of the costs of elementary and secondary education across Maine by 2008-2009 in an effort to fairly balance the local cost burden among Maine's school districts. The goal was right: a strong education for every child in Maine, regardless of where he or she lived or parents' means. Behind the 55% promise was an implicit recognition that Maine is one community of only 1,300,000 people.

Maine has never kept its promise. The state's share has slipped below 45%, the lowest it has been since LD 1 was enacted.

The state's failure to keep its promise has meant a massive shift in the responsibility for funding education from the statewide tax base to local property taxes in Maine's cities and towns. Because Maine's cities and towns have no significant source of funds other than the unfair and regressive property tax, the state's failure has advantaged wealthier communities and those with higher property values and/or fewer school-age children, while less affluent communities with more children and service center cities with large amounts of tax-exempt property have been penalized.

The time has come to reexamine the way we fund public education in Maine and to consider – in conjunction with a thorough reform of Maine's taxation structure – whether a broader base for funding public education makes good sense.

If we assumed a broader state responsibility for funding local education (and lived up to it), could we (a) maintain local control of schools while (b) creating equal opportunities for all Maine kids and (c) providing incentives for school districts to innovate, share services and put their school facilities to broader community uses? It's something we need to talk about as we work to make all Maine kids better trained and better educated.

6. Lower Costs for Higher Education

An increasingly expensive public system of post-secondary education has both discouraged many graduating high school seniors from continuing their education in Maine and has driven more high school seniors to colleges and universities outside Maine, taking knowledge and innovation with them. This is unacceptable.

According to the Georgetown University Center on Education and the Workforce, nearly 60% of Maine jobs will require training and formal education beyond high school by 2018, and over 40% of those will require either a two- or four-year degree. Today, though, slightly more than a third of Maine's high student graduates go on to earn a college degree, a rate lower than the U.S. average and the lowest in New England.

As well, graduation rates from universities within the University of Maine System are unacceptably low.[28] An undereducated workforce will have an overwhelmingly negative impact on incomes in Maine – individually and on a statewide basis.

Overcoming Maine's post-secondary education deficit (including two-year and four-year college and post-high school skills education) is one of the most critical tasks facing our state today. The shortcomings in Maine's job market and the consequent

---

[28] From the Bangor Daily News, July 17, 2013, "*The Wasted Potential at Maine's Universities*," by Stephen Weber, former president of San Diego State University: "[T]he University of Maine System's six-year graduation rates (the national standard of comparison) are as follows: Orono, 60.4 percent; Southern Maine, 32.9 percent; Augusta, 16 percent; Farmington, 59.4 percent; Fort Kent, 33.3 percent; Machias 37.7 percent; and Presque Isle, 29.8 percent, according to the Education Trust."

deterioration in our incomes won't be fixed until we invest in post-secondary education – both academic and vocational – in a strategic, focused, consistent and sustained way.

Part of the problem is money, but there's more to it than that. Maine's problems also flow from a balkanized system of public higher education management, one that discourages cooperation and too often serves only the narrowest interests. Net expenditures for public higher education are low in Maine in comparison to the rest of the nation, yet Maine has the one of the nation's highest non-instructional payrolls relative to instructional payrolls.

We need to make major investments in Maine's higher education physical plant; the levels of deferred maintenance and necessary facilities replacement on our public campuses rival the challenges in Maine's system of roads and bridges. But no amount of public investment in the systems' facilities will increase the affordability of post-secondary education for Maine high school graduates. Before we make those investments, we need to get our arms around the systems' costs.

We should start by merging our university and college systems into one system that costs less to operate and consequently makes available more money to invest in actual education.

At a time of massive cost impediments to education access, and in a small state that is by almost any measure one of the most fiscally challenged in America, Maine boasts post-secondary education programs on 14 different college and university campuses, at 17 outreach centers and in about 75 other learning sites. In part, this extraordinary proliferation of programs and sites has come to pass because Maine has tolerated for too long an organizational framework that is ill-designed to achieve strategic decision-making, coordination and the disciplined allocation of resources.

One governing body for both systems should improve efficiency and planning for the various campuses and reduce unnecessary duplication of programs. One central office for planning and administration should mean closer collaboration among the community colleges and four-year university campuses in sequenced, affordable programs in a variety of specialized programs.

At the same time, accessibility to courses needs to be improved, allowing students to more easily make continuing progress toward degree completion.[29]

---

[29] Recent efforts by the Legislature, supported by the presidents of the University of Maine System and the Maine Community College System, to facilitate students' transfer of credits earned on one campus to another, as well as between the respective systems, are an important step in the right direction, and are long overdue.

In a new funding and management environment, campuses will no longer duplicate programs in an effort to expand enrollments; such strategies too often result in too few students in programs with too few qualified faculty, with the net result of weakening the entire system.

Extra-system MOOCs (massive online open enrollment courses) intra-system distance learning through the use of broadband technology can dramatically increase access a lower costs, while "hybrid" courses, using a combination of MOOC or distance learning and face-to-face, real–time contact with a local instructor can often result in more effective instruction than either distance or in-person instruction alone.

We should make the best use of all of Maine's post-secondary assets, by creating a Center for Professional Graduate Education, by achieving closer coordination with Maine's K-12 systems and by instituting additional magnet high schools on or near college campuses.

Once we have made the kinds of organizational changes that are necessary to bring the size, shape and cost of our public post-secondary education system into line with what Maine needs and what Maine can afford – but not before – we should commence a 10-year program of sustained reinvestment in that system and in its physical facilities.

Finally, Maine should consider implementing "Pay It Forward, Pay It Back," the plan in place in Australia and just approved for study in Oregon that creates a fund to support tuition-free post-high school education. Maine high school graduates could attend Maine's public colleges and universities on a tuition-free basis, on the condition that they live and work in Maine and pay the fund back with a nominal percentage of their income over 20-25 years following graduation.

If we can keep and employ in Maine most of the 400,000 people under the age of 25 now living here, they will become the greatest resource for the future prosperity of our state. To make Maine smarter, we will need to make investments with a long-term focus. We will need to strengthen every school, empower every teacher and principal, and better prepare every child.

7

Smarter Government:
Wise and Prudent, Fair and Efficient

- Maine people deserve a government that is responsive, efficient and creative.

- We can replace sticks with carrots. Targeted incentives can help identify ways to combine local services at real savings for taxpayers.

- A Cleanup Commission should review all state programs and agencies and ask the legislature for an up or down vote on ways to make state government more innovative, more efficient and less costly.

- An Office of The Grim Repealer should review rules and regulations to help the governor and the legislature get rid of those that are unnecessary, counter-productive, inefficient and ineffective.

- Maine's outmoded, inefficient, highly regressive and unfair tax structure stands in the way of sustained economic growth, more jobs and shared prosperity. It needs to be fixed and revamped so that it raises the money government needs in ways that are fair and smart.

Maine people want a state government that is smart, entrepreneurial and effective, and they want to pay for it with taxes that are fair, equitable and efficient. They want their leaders at both the state and federal level to focus on solutions, not on scoring political victories. They want a plan to grow Maine's economy that makes sense for their kids' futures.

Where government is broken, our task should be to fix it, not kill it.

Governor Andrew Cuomo of New York recently said it well: ". . .[W]hat politics is about today is a very simple formula – demonstrate government competence and capacity, that government can actually work, that it can do something efficiently and effectively, that it's not gridlocked, and it's not incompetent."

That's really not a high hurdle. Our expectations of government (perhaps tempered by too many years of failures) are pretty basic. Much of what ails government has less to do with what it tries to do than it does with the ways in which it tries to do it.

1. Carrots, not Sticks

No one likes being told what to do, and that goes double for Mainers. Few state policies have elicited more argument and anger than the compulsory school consolidation plan enacted in 2007 that penalized communities that failed to combine with others.

At the same time, it is clear to most of us that an aging population, declining school enrollments and increasing costs and salaries mean that in many parts of Maine school systems may be overbuilt and overstaffed.

Similarly, smaller hospitals, particularly in rural Maine, are cutting back the services they provide, leaving many of us worried about access to preventive and emergency care.

As noted, Maine supports a state university system with seven campuses and dozens of satellite facilities, plus seven community colleges in an entirely separate system, to serve a population of only 1,300,000 people.

Finally, there isn't one Maine taxpayer who hasn't at some point wondered whether it's really necessary for towns and cities located a stone's throw across a bridge from each other – think Bangor and Brewer, Waterville and Winslow, Lewiston and Auburn, Portland and South Portland, Biddeford and Saco – to duplicate most city services.

Real progress has been made in recent years in breaking down artificial barriers and gaining economies of scale, but there is much more that we can and ought to do, and the State should offer powerful incentives – considerably more attractive than penalties – that could light the way.

Delivering public services in efficient and cost-effective ways does not need to mean – and must not mean – the destruction of local communities; indeed, if we are smart about it, we can strengthen and enhance the vitality of communities while we improve and make more efficient the delivery of government services in ways that end up costing us less.

For example, schools (or even parts of schools) that no longer are needed in cities and towns across Maine can be repurposed as community services centers, providing close-to-home video links to state and local service agencies; through collaboration with Maine's hospital systems, providing access to preventive health counseling and urgent care, including telemedicine portals that link patients directly with providers in distant medical centers; recreation facilities; and high-quality video connections to massive open online course offerings (MOOCs), extension services and adult and continuing education courses.

It is squarely in the interests of the state government to provide incentives to local communities to consolidate and improve access to public services, because, if it's done right, the state government (and state taxpayers) will save money in lower operating costs. One way that the state can provide incentives, of course, would be to help pay the upfront capital costs of facilities conversion and new equipment. Another would be through tax-based incentives (more on that later). In either case, though, the requirements need to be flexible; the savings and rewards need to be real; and we can't expect it all to happen overnight.

2. Clean 'em Up, Shut 'em Down

Any chief executive, whether in the public or the private sector, will tell you that the two achievements that give her or him more of a sense of accomplishment than anything else are these: one, shutting down a program or wiping a statute or regulation off the books that doesn't work or no longer is needed; and two, starting a new product or activity that is needed, that does work and that customers buy or voters and citizens appreciate.

Too many times in recent years in Maine we've gotten it upside down. That is, our state government has gone off in pursuit of "solutions" that we don't need, that won't work and that most Mainers think are crazy; cramming state responsibilities down the pipe to local governments by tax-shifting is a good recent example. Meanwhile, we've left in place agencies, statutes and rules that at best waste money and at worst do real damage.

Cleaning up the government isn't as easy as cleaning out our closets or getting rid of "the pile," because it not only takes time but also, in many cases, entails real political risk for legislators (and governors) who understandably aren't eager to take risk.

Here are some ways to tackle these housecleaning jobs that I think will work and that we ought to try.

SMACC

Government reorganizations, where agencies and departments are merged and boxes are moved around on pieces of paper, often cost more money than they save. But when you get rid of something – a military base or a government program or department – you can begin to save real money.

If the legislature will authorize it, the governor ought to personally chair a commission that would operate in a way similar to the Base Realignment and Closure Commission (BRAC) process where the federal government determines which military bases to keep or to close. The State of Maine Cleanup Commission (call it SMACC) would review state programs and agencies, and within a year would make a series of recommendations to make state government more innovative, more efficient and less costly. The governor would present those recommendations to the Legislature as a single package, and legislators would need to cast a "yes or no" vote on the entire package. There will be less temptation to vote "no," just to preserve a favorite agency or program, and lots of shared rewards for voting "yes."

Office of The Grim Repealer

Like most states, Maine has thousands of rules flowing from statutes and regulations enacted or promulgated over many decades. Taken together they are complicated, confusing, and – due to the law of unintended consequences – often counterproductive when measured against our aspirations for a clean, competitive state economy with a strong sense of community. Many of these regulations were drafted to serve a narrow purpose that no longer exists, and many have been rendered out of date by changes in the world around us.

Maine's governor could establish a small, one or two-person Office of Regulatory Review and Repeal (ORRR). The head of the ORRR – (call her or him The Grim Repealer) – would report directly to the governor and would have two principal responsibilities: first, review Maine rules and regulations to identify those that are unnecessary, counterproductive, inefficient and ineffective – or just don't work the way they should and should be repealed or modified; and second, review rules and regulations that agencies and departments propose, before they take effect, to ensure that they will accomplish their purposes in the most efficient and least costly and disruptive ways.

We'll find many examples of redundancies and poorly tailored efforts that can either be eliminated or improved. In many cases, the rules can be repealed or modified by agency or executive order. Where the approval of the legislature is required, the changes could be considered together as part of the SMACC package or separately.

This office should also engage the talents of those who are on the cutting edge of developing "apps" and related tools to take a fresh look at how we do things and to suggest efficiencies, enhancements and service improvements that can be created through the smart application of technology.

3. Fair and Equitable Taxes

Standing between Maine and sustained economic growth, more jobs and shared prosperity is an outmoded, inefficient, highly regressive and unfair tax structure.

For local jurisdictions in Maine the property tax is the only meaningful revenue-raising mechanism to fund the operating and capital costs of local government, including police and fire protection, local roads, schools and other municipal and county services.

As a revenue source, the property tax is highly stressed. Local governments have only the property tax to fall back on when state funding for public education is insufficient, when municipal revenue sharing is slashed, or when tough winters wreak havoc with local roads and increase the costs of plowing, sand and salt.

The property tax is also regressive. The tax was introduced in America during colonial times, when the wealth of most Americans, affluent or not, was concentrated in real property. Today, in our modern economy, the wealth of the richest Mainers no longer is concentrated in their holdings of real property; instead, vastly greater amounts of their wealth are invested in stocks and bonds and a wide range of other assets, none of which are taxed except when they generate income or are passed on to heirs. For Maine citizens of less means and affluence, though, real property – their homes remain their principal and sometimes only investment, so their taxes are assessed against a much higher percentage of their wealth than in the cases of their more affluent neighbors.

Maine cities' and towns' increasing dependence on the property tax hurts Maine in several ways:

- PreK-12 students in property- and income-poor towns deserve just as much opportunity as their peers in neighboring, wealthier communities, but don't have it – and it is just as unfair at the same time to seniors living on fixed incomes.

- Communities are pitted against each other in efforts to attract commercial development, creating more sprawl and increasing the costs of delivering services.

- The tax drives farmers from the land and fishermen from the shore, putting at risk those very Maine communities that are the backbone of our tourist economy.

- Service center cities and towns that provide municipal services to people who don't live there are limited in their ability to raise revenues to provide those services by high concentrations of hospitals, churches, colleges and other tax-exempt property.

- Too often and in too many places, particularly with the slow death of revenue sharing, the property tax doesn't raise enough revenue to provide state local governments the money they need to meet needs for public services, to fix our roads and to invest in our children's futures.

The Maine sales tax is also unfair and regressive, by virtue of a base that is narrower than in most other states and excludes many discretionary services and expensive recreational pursuits. All of us buy groceries and medicine (which generally are not currently taxed) and clothes and other durable goods (which generally are), but some services and leisure activities are for the most part purchased by those at the higher ends of the wealth and income scale. Broadening the sales tax base to include a wider range of services and eliminating a large number of sales tax exemptions would be a step in the right direction.

Maine's estate tax is badly out of conformity with the federal estate tax, while Maine's income tax rates remain too high, particularly for moderate income Mainers. (Nonetheless, the suggestion that the income tax could be entirely eliminated amounts to unsupportable political blather.)

Finally, a discussion on Maine taxes would be incomplete without noting the fact that we effectively spend in Maine hundreds of millions of dollars every year that are not collected because of tax breaks, deductions and credits. Economists and government wonks call these tax expenditures. That spending isn't mentioned in the governor's budget proposal, and the legislature never considers and appropriates it in the biennial budget, but those tax breaks increase the tax burden on taxpayers on a dollar-for-dollar basis.

That kind of backdoor spending might be tolerable, if we were confident that all of those tax breaks were accomplishing important objectives ... but we can't be confident, because we don't know. Many of those tax breaks were enacted years ago for purposes that seemed important at the time and that perhaps we could then afford. But for the most part, they've been on autopilot; most have never been closely evaluated to see if they're still working, still needed and still accomplishing their goals (if they ever did). At the very least, they should be identified in our budget as expenditures that, rightly or wrongly, we have chosen to make and that we need to examine.

No one likes taxes, but most of us are willing to pay taxes if we believe that they are fair and necessary. Taxes should raise the least amount of money we need in Maine for public services and investment, in ways that are fair and equitable. Our tax policies should promote opportunity without seeking to engineer particular results or to advance or advantage narrow economic agendas.

One of our top priorities in a plan for Maine should be to reform Maine's tax structure – all of it – in ways that will help us leverage our competitive advantages, create and protect opportunity, and grow our economy.

8
Stronger Economy: Investing in Maine's Competitive Advantages

- No state can match our extraordinary combination of natural resources, location and quality of life.

- We should invest in a serious and sustained way in the development of an umbrella Maine brand that can be an enduring economic driver even in challenging economic times.

- A focused effort to leverage Maine's competitive advantages can generate jobs and increase incomes. Our future growth will be driven by agriculture, by tourism and by the arts, manufacturing and research sectors of the creative economy.

- Wise decisions about capital investments – choosing among compelling needs for spending on infrastructure repair and human capital development – will require a capital budget and a capital budgeting process. Well-run businesses have capital budgeting processes, and so should the State of Maine.

One day a year or so ago, a fellow in Dover-Foxcroft who is about my age asked me this question:

> "Our fathers and mothers fought a world war, came home and built roads and bridges and schools, educated you and me and our friends. They made investments for us. They didn't ask us, when we were three years old, whether we wanted to make those investments; they just went out and did it, with their money, because they knew it was the right thing to do for us. What are we doing for our kids?"

Good question. It's hard to come up with a good answer, because we're not investing enough, and we're certainly not investing enough in Maine's competitive advantages.

When my partner and I decided to start our own business 25 years ago, we faced a choice between (a) competing with other law firms by offering just as many services, albeit at lower prices, or (b) competing in fewer areas where we knew that we could offer higher quality services without compromising on price.

We decided at the outset to focus nearly exclusively on what we did better than other law firms, which was solving environmental and land use issues that arise in big public infrastructure projects like airports, highways and Superfund sites. It turned out to be the right decision, because our law firm grew to become the second largest environmental law firm in America. I believe we were successful in large part because we never strayed from our focus on our competitive advantage.

As we plot a strategy to strengthen Maine's economy by leveraging Maine's competitive advantages, we, too, need to steer clear of two traps that have snagged us in the in the past – pipe dreams and bargain pricing.

A lot of dreaming and wishful thinking crops up in conversations about how to grow Maine's economy. Some of those dreams are worth pursuing, but many aren't.

Mayor Michael Brennan's proposal for a Portland-area research campus like North Carolina's Research Triangle Park, for example, would capitalize on Maine's competitive advantages – that Maine is a place where talented people want to live, that we have a big and highly regarded medical center in southern Maine, that Maine has strengths in life sciences, and that the products of brainpower can be transmitted instantly and inexpensively to any place in the world. Investing in that dream would make sense, because it would be an investment in Maine's competitive advantages.

But dreams also can be pipe dreams that lead us to invest in the wrong places, and Maine needs to be prudent and careful about where we invest.

Another big mistake we sometimes make is bargain pricing, where we mimic a surplus store and adopt a shortsighted focus on price over quality. We need to keep in mind that in most cases where we have little or no natural competitive advantage, we will never win a competitive pricing battle with other states, because too many factors work against us.

Mainers need to remember that no state can match our extraordinary combination of natural resources and location or the quality of life that we have to sell. Lowering the costs of doing business in Maine – particularly health care and education – should be a key objective in any plan for economic development, as it is in the one presented in this book, but we must also invest in Maine's strengths in order to preserve them.

Those are *our* strengths, Maine's competitive advantages. We needn't be cheap in areas where we're the best.

Virtually every natural trend evident in the world today is working to Maine's advantage.

- In a world increasingly short of freshwater, Maine has enormous amounts of it that are renewed every year.

- In a world where fossil fuels are increasingly hard to extract in cost-effective and environmentally sensible ways, and where burning them is more and more problematic, Maine gets more sun than Germany, the world's leader in solar energy, while Maine's onshore and offshore wind energy resources are endlessly renewable and increasingly cost-competitive in life-cycle terms.

- In a world where food that is sustainably grown with traceable origins is increasingly prized, the products of Maine's farms and fisheries can command premium prices.

- In a world where aging populations have higher disposable incomes and want to see the world, Maine's natural splendor is a priceless resource.

- In a world where more and more goods are shipped between continents by ocean freight, the opening of the Inside Passage to commercial shipping will make Eastport *the* deep water U.S. port (without the need for expensive dredging) with the shortest combined distances to America's largest transocean trading partners – China, Japan, Korea and the European Union.

So with the wind at our backs, how can we make the most of our competitive advantages? How can we leverage Maine's spectacular resources into more and better jobs and higher incomes?

What do we need to do? What's the plan?

1. Unlock Value, Jobs and Income from Maine's Natural Resources.

The good news about Maine's renewable natural resources – our assets that undergird both the tourism industry in Maine and so many of our other important industries – is that for the most part they are healthy, and the parts of the economy that they support are reasonably strong. Though employment declined dramatically in most sectors of the forest products sector during the Lost Decade, production levels have remained high.[30]

Although lower wages in Asia and unfair foreign competition have disadvantaged Maine and America, the biggest reason behind the dramatic decline in the number of employees has been the productivity gains generated by rapidly advancing technology. There is nothing on the horizon that would suggest that advances in technology won't continue to eat away at employment opportunities in many of Maine's traditional industries. Moreover, increasingly mobile capital migrates easily to lower-cost environments, and it is easier and easier to move products manufactured in those lower cost environments to global markets.

These trends don't favor the production of commodity-grade products in Maine and other places that will continue to face tough competition – if not with Asia today, then with Africa down the road – even as we make every effort to overcome them.

However, these trends also explain why important elements of Maine forest products and other natural resources sectors can continue to thrive.

Although papermaking jobs declined, employment in fishing, farming, forestry and logging remained relatively steady during the 2000-2011 period, This strength didn't begin to make up for the jobs and wages that Maine lost to productivity gains in the paper and wood products industries, but points the way to future growth and success. These sectors of our economy remain vital and should be targeted not only for production gains, but for more jobs and higher wages as well.

Agriculture offers a compelling picture of a sector of the Maine economy where there is great potential and no plan.

Farming is both central to our Maine heritage and can leverage big competitive advantages – plenty of water and arable land and proximity to affluent markets. Moreover, the more farms we have and the more local food we produce, the more good restau-

---

[30] Jobs in paper and wood products manufacturing fell from approximately 20,000 in 2000 to about 11,500 in 2011, even though Maine continues to produce lumber, pulp and paper at historically high levels. (For comparison, Maine's tourism industry supports about 85,500 jobs.)

rants they supply and the more attractive a place Maine is for tourists to visit, helping to build Maine's brand.

According to the Maine Farmland Trust, there were 6.5 million acres under cultivation in Maine in 1880, when our state was a breadbasket for the northeastern United States. Today there are only 1.3 million cultivated acres – merely 20% of what we once had – even though transportation and technology have brought the northeastern markets much closer to us than they were 135 years ago.

Acreage under cultivation in Maine is slowly growing again, generating jobs and incomes, but agriculture is not growing nearly as rapidly as it could if Maine were following a strategy to encourage it and put in place the right policies to make it happen.

Many of Maine's new farmers are young and educated; indeed, in a state that is the oldest in America and is aging faster than any other state, some have suggested that Maine's population of farmers is among the youngest in America. Here's a place where inventive public policies – focused on attracting young people to Maine to farm and helping them finance their entrepreneurial efforts – should both leverage competitive advantages and help turn around Maine's demographic disadvantage.

2. Build and Develop the Maine Brand.

Maine businesses can succeed with grown, harvested and manufactured products like high quality foods from year-round agriculture; kelp, seaweed, mussels and lobster products; coated and specialty papers; and handcrafted furniture. These products from our natural resources will command higher prices because they possess unique qualities that can't be duplicated elsewhere.

These Maine businesses will find even greater success if we create and develop an umbrella Maine brand that builds markets and drives demand for products from our renewable resources (from food to pulp to tourism).

Maine's image as a beautiful, rock solid, safe and altogether genuine location is a marketer's dream. Successful Maine companies like L.L.Bean, Tom's of Maine and Poland Spring have managed to incorporate into their products, or into the communications surrounding their products, many of the qualities associated with the Maine brand.

Consumers around the world – whether boat buyers or tourists looking for new experiences – are willing to pay for the higher quality and unique characteristics of products and experiences associated and marked with brands that they know and respect.

Maine ought to be just such a brand. The Maine brand can be – should be – an enduring economic driver even in challenging economic times. The latent power of the Maine brand is extraordinary; there are only a few states that are mythic, and Maine is one of them. We need to make that hidden potential real.

Building a powerful brand for our state is both an investment opportunity and an obligation that we have ignored for decades. For a state where so many jobs – now and in the future – are and will be found in tourism and in other areas of the creative economy, there aren't many more important investments that we can make in our future and in our kids' futures than the development of a strong Maine brand.

If Virginia can be for lovers (as it has been for decades), if you and I can love New York, if pork can be the new white meat... then we ought to be able to figure out how we want people to think about Maine, and then get them to think that way.

What will draw people to insist on buying our lobsters, rather than ones from Canada?

What will cause new Chinese customers to buy boats or furniture made in Maine instead of boats and furniture made in Italy?

What will motivate people to want to live here so much that they'll move their businesses here?

What do we want potential visitors or would-be neighbors to think about us, about who we are, what we make, what it's like to visit Maine or to live among us?

Maine's brand confusion is painfully evident in one of our most important industries. Over the years Maine's tourism promotion efforts have veered from one slogan to another faster than our weather changes. We're *"Vacationland"* on our license plates, while our slogans have gone in recent years from *"The way life should be"* to *"It Must Be Maine,"* the latter tag prompting Business Week analysts to observe that Maine's brand "isn't well-known because [the slogan] is bland, dreary, and vague."

Now Maine's slogan is *"The Maine Thing."* Maybe "The Maine Thing" is a slogan that conveys to some people the beauty of Maine and the quality of what we make and do... but it's brand-building potential seems remote.

We don't have everything wrong; there are now, for instance, some appealing new videos on the Maine tourism web site where Maine folks talk about why we all love to live here. But there is no evidence that we have invested the kind of time, effort, expertise and... yes... money that can develop a brand that is meaningful, a true umbrella brand that embraces all of the products and experiences for which we want Maine to be known, one that motivates people to place a higher value on what we make and sell and on the experience of living and visiting here.

The development of a permanent, iconic, umbrella Maine brand should be one of our first top-level objectives, because it is more than just a slogan to attract tourists. A Maine brand may be one of the most valuable shared, public assets that we can create. Maine needs to claim its place on the map of the world; it's just not enough anymore for Maine to have a place in our hearts. We need to develop a Maine brand that connotes and embodies the Maine experience in all of its diverse forms.

Whether it is our paper and wood products, our lobster, our blueberries, our native-raised and spun wool and wool products, our Maine-built boats or our Maine-inspired and produced art, music and literature, we should aggressively build and promote a single unified Maine brand and strategically seek markets— an audience–for products that are authentically and indisputably Maine-made, grown or produced.

3. Promote Year-Round, Destination and Cultural Tourism

No industry is more important to Maine's future than tourism. It is our biggest industry and, by some measures, one of our fastest growing business sectors. At roughly $7.5 billion annually, the industry represents about 10% of our current GDP and a huge potential source of meaningful economic growth as more baby boomers around the world retire to lives of travel, adventure and cultural exploration.

Lasting and meaningful growth in the Maine economy – more jobs and higher incomes – will be hard to come by in the absence of real growth in Maine's number one industry. On the other hand, dramatic increases in year-round, destination and cultural tourism would fuel not only annual increases in the volume of tourists but also increases in the amounts of spending per tourist visit. With increases in tourist spending will come better-paying jobs in Maine's tourism economy.

Unlike many of Maine's traditional industries, tourism is helped, not threatened, by new technology, and lower labor costs in places like Bangladesh and Vietnam have no impact whatsoever on its viability. The same demographics that plague us in other ways – as the oldest and fastest aging population in America – work to our advantage in tourism, as older and more affluent people across America and around the world want to travel and visit places like Maine.

Yet, in terms of its contributions to Maine tax revenues and to Maine jobs and incomes, the sector is an underperformer. More visitors to Maine are making increasing demands on our infrastructure and services while spending less money during their stays. From 2011 to 2012, for example, total visitation to Maine increased by 8.5%, but direct tourist expenditures increased by only 0.9%, tax revenues from tourism increased by only 0.8% and both jobs and earnings in the tourist sector *declined*.

Maine's natural resources and welcoming communities give us an enormous competitive advantage in the tourism marketplace, but we can do a much better job of leveraging that competitive advantage. A big part of a plan for Maine should be helping the Maine tourism industry derive a better return from Maine's extraordinary tourism assets.

As with the rest of our natural resources economy, tourism is an export business; here, the export product is experience and, given our location and our market, the mode of export is typically a family automobile. Deriving higher value from exports of the Maine experience will require building the Maine brand, developing higher value products that make better, more year-round use of our assets, and broadening the markets from which we draw our visitors. More destination experiences, year-round activities and cultural tourism would drive higher returns on our tourism asset base, more jobs and higher incomes.

There are certainly positive signs out there. The Riverfront Concerts in Bangor have become a summertime destination experience, with a $30 million economic impact in a region much bigger than just Bangor, and the Maine Huts and Trails development serves both the destination experience objective and improves four-season access to the Maine woods.

But we need to do more, much more. Out of 100 results from a recent Google search for "museum tours in Maine," for example, the only thing that turned up was a Smithsonian tour in August, 2013 that visited but two of Maine's many great museums. That's not good.

A prospective cultural tourist to Maine should be able to easily find a guided tour that visits the Ogunquit Museum of Art; the Portland Museum of Art; the Bates, Bowdoin, Colby and University of Maine and University of New England museums; the Farnsworth Museum in Rockland; the Maine Maritime Museum in Bath; and the Penobscot Marine Museum in Searsport.

An inventive and entrepreneurial tour operator could couple those museum visits with visits to Acadia and Baxter Parks; some of our other glorious state parks; overnight stays at charming hotels, inns and B & B's; and meals at some of the best farm-to-table restaurants in America. Throw in some snowmobiling or skiing in the winter and beaches and mountain climbing in the summer; visits to Bath Iron Works, art galleries and boatyards; outlet shopping, concerts and evenings with Maine authors talking about their books – and before long you have a compelling offering that should draw more higher-spending tourists to Maine.

One of the great strengths of Maine's tourism industry is that it is a big collection of small businesses, but that characteristic can at the same time make it difficult to focus industry attention on new efforts to develop year-round, cultural and destination tourism, or to marshal the collective efforts needed to develop and promote important collaboration among places, regions and resources in a highly fragmented industry.

The Maine Office of Tourism, the Maine Tourism Association and groups of owners and operators like the Maine Innkeepers and the Maine Restaurant Association work hard at promoting Maine's biggest industry, but they are constrained by limited development and promotion budgets in a highly competitive marketplace. Increasing the size of Maine's tourism sector will require attention, leadership and a sustained financial commitment from the State of Maine. It is also time we recognized the importance of tourism to Maine by re-naming the Department of Economic and Community Development the Department of Commerce and Tourism.

Finally, we need to pay as much attention to the preservation of Maine's special community resources as we have paid to preserving our mountains, lakes and coastal views. One of the important objectives in a plan for Maine's future needs to be the preservation of the rural Maine farming, North Woods and coastal communities that give Maine's tourism assets depth and character that are unmatched anywhere in the world.

4. Invigorate and Support the Creative Economy – in Arts, Research and Manufacturing

The creative economy is not just about the production and consumption of visual and performing arts, it is about the unique and innovative ideas, technologies and output of virtually every sector of our economy, and it is one of the keys to Maine's future growth.

The creative economy engine can generate real prosperity. Mark Bessire, the director of the Portland Museum of Art, put it well. Whether it's about boats, art, furniture, paper, food, museums or restaurants, he said, "people come to Maine to be creative." And, not incidentally, most of those who come are young.

Our thinking about "creative economy" too frequently relegates creative endeavor to a rarified niche of academia, museums, galleries and performance halls. Particularly in Maine, our understanding of "creative economy" should encompass much more than the traditional mix of the visual and performing arts. Maine workers are known to be skilled, innovative, creative and adept at meeting manufacturing challenges. In a similar vein, Maine's unique quality of place rests not only on our unparalleled natural beauty and its conservation and our culture of historic towns and their preservation; our quality of place also has much to do with who we are – the creative workforce that produces our unique artistic, manufactured, technological, agricultural, and aquatic products.

One of the best examples of the importance of recognizing and adopting this broader definition is acknowledging and emphasizing in our strategy for growth the importance of particular research and manufacturing sectors to Maine's economy. For example, Maine-built boats remain known and valued all over the world, from the largest Navy vessels built at Bath Iron Works to the smallest skiffs and sailboats built at boatyards along the length of the Maine coast.

Four of the seven largest private manufacturing employers in Maine reside in a broadly defined precision manufacturing sector. Beyond those giants, Maine is dotted with dozens of small precision manufacturers in the electronics, machining and tool making sectors. And we need to keep our eyes open for other opportunities to bring manufacturing back to Maine – in the fashioning of garments from native fibres, for example.

Maine also is seeing significant opportunities in the development of new composite fuels and materials, including encouraging prospects for harnessing Maine's natural resources, that are emerging from labs at the University of Maine. Exciting and groundbreaking research is underway at the University of New England, Maine's medical centers, the Jackson and Bigelow laboratories, the Gulf of Maine Research Institute and scores of other public and private institutions.

Over the last decade, a multitude of studies and papers generated by both public and private institutions have explored the creative economy in Maine with the aim of understanding the nature, impact and growth potential for arts, entertainment, recreation and technology, and how to foster that growth as a focus of state policy. It's time to take the best of those studies' recommendations off the shelf and to make them part of a serious and focused plan to build Maine's creative economy.

- Making healthcare and education more accessible and less costly in Maine is the most important first step in this direction, as are targeted efforts to attract educated and skilled young people to Maine.

- Sustained efforts to attract and assist artists and creative entrepreneurs are essential. State government can help strengthen and coordinate the efforts of Creative Portland and other public and private sector groups throughout Maine that are actively fostering visible arts districts in our larger towns and cities, affordable workspaces and housing.

- The State of Maine can work with banks, credit unions and foundations to promote favorable financing for creative endeavors, including the bricks and mortar needed to house them.

- By creating clear pathways from middle schools to university and community college STEM education and training, Maine can insure that the state's *future* workforce is as well educated in science, technology, engineering and math (the STEM areas) as the employment opportunities in this sector will require.

- Pre-K through high school education in the arts can help Maine produce the artists, performers, writers, designers, architects, boat builders, chefs, artisanal food producers, vintners, and other creative small business entrepreneurs who make Maine a magnet for year-round tourism, who create the products for our global markets, and whose success in greater numbers will help lift all of Maine. Maine could create a magnet arts high school to do for the creative arts what the magnet school in Limestone is doing for science and technology education with remarkable success.

5. Use a Capital Budget to Make Investment Decisions

When it comes to making major investment decisions in Maine, we often find ourselves stunned by public policies that would never pass muster in our households or businesses.

I left the Democratic Party in 2004, among other reasons because Maine's governor at the time sought to borrow money for the *wrong* purposes – essentially to pay part of the state's annual operating expenses. In 2011 and 2012 today's governor refused to borrow and invest for the *right* purposes at a time when interest rates were at historic lows.

The State of Maine's ratio of bonded indebtedness to GDP is lower than the ratio in every other New England state and lower than the national average. Maine's needs for capital investment are compelling. So, at a time when interest rates were lower than they likely will ever again be in our lifetimes, why did Maine's leaders refuse to borrow money – except for $100 million to build a new prison that nobody knew we needed?

Why? In part because Maine doesn't have a reliably functioning and rigorously analytic capital budgeting process, one that compares on a continuing basis capital investment candidates (roads, bridges, prison and university buildings, land purchases, and so on).

A good capital budgeting process *might* have yielded as a top priority a brand new prison, but probably not. A good capital budgeting process *would* replace the often but not always well-informed whims of the governor and the legislature with analyses of levels of need and potential returns on investment, arraying choices in a systematic and useful way for the governor, the legislature and Maine citizens (who vote in referenda to approve or reject the borrowing). Importantly, a capital budgeting process would also help ensure that Maine makes capital investments when it makes good sense to do so, instead of passing on golden opportunities in slavish obedience to political dogma or to score partisan political points.

Our state and local governments are the only instruments we have for making investments in public facilities and public needs for which no company or individual or charity can be expected to take responsibility. These facilities and needs – ranging from roads, bridges, ports and railroads to public education to sewage treatment plants to parks – are both necessary elements of our communities' daily existence and critical building blocks for a growing economy that produces jobs and incomes. Indeed, we waste our opportunities when we fail to make these investments.

Some communities will move ahead on their own. The people of Eastport created and empowered a port authority that could invest public energies and resources in the development of the town's single biggest competitive advantage, its deep water port.

The State of Maine needs to assess statewide needs from a statewide perspective. Just how great is the potential for Eastport's deep water harbor as the Inside Passage opens and as other east coast ports become more crowded, more congested – and no closer to our trading partners? Could it become an important transshipment hub, as well as a port that allows more Maine products to be efficiently exported to parts of the world like China where demand is growing and domestic supplies are constrained?

Maine needs a capital budget and a capital budgeting process. It's past time. Maine's current infrastructure investment policies could not be more at odds with our best bets for economic growth.

6. Make Investments in Assets That Enhance Competitive Advantage

Once a sound capital budgeting process is in place, a plan for Maine should include a schedule of investments in public assets that will most help to leverage our competitive advantages.

If the Port of Eastport could likely have a substantial impact on the economy of Washington County and all of eastern Maine, then perhaps the state – all of us – should invest in the development of a rail connection to the port.

The same kinds of questions need to be asked – and answered – about roads and bridges. Today's levels of state and federal highway funds aren't sufficient to keep current on maintenance and to undertake needed major repairs. Sooner or later, Maine's tourism industry and other exporters will pay the price exacted by a crumbling infrastructure.

There is no industry with more statewide importance than tourism. It's Maine's largest and most important industry, with approximately $7.5 billion in annual economic impact and 85,000 jobs that pay more than $2.2 billion in yearly wages. Most tourists arrive in Maine and travel around Maine by automobile – over our bridges and on our roads.

Maine's rural roads (14th from the bottom) and bridges (12th from the bottom) are now ranked among the worst in the country, and Maine's entire highway infrastructure just received a D grade from the American Society of Civil Engineers. The best available estimates say that we will need to spend about $3.3 billion in the next several years to bring our roads and bridges up to snuff.

Apart from the adverse impact on tourism, the condition of our roads and bridges is costing every Mainer more to operate his or her vehicle than it should – and more than it costs drivers in other states. Maine drivers each spend about $300 a year in additional operating costs due to deteriorated roads. And the problem is likely to get worse before it gets better, as projections predict a 20% increase in vehicle miles traveled over Maine roads during the next 17 years.

As the roads get more battered, the money available from existing revenue sources to fix them is evaporating. Revenue projections for the state's highway fund are heading in the wrong direction; the state gasoline tax hasn't been raised, other than to track inflation, since 1997, and indexing was ended altogether in 2012. As cars are becoming more and more fuel-efficient, total revenues from the gasoline tax are trending down. Moreover, there is little likelihood that federal funding for roads and bridges will recover to earlier levels.

So Maine's options are limited. One alternative is sit on our hands, make no investments in our future, allow our infrastructure to deteriorate even more, watch tourists go elsewhere, and eventually wonder why our economy is trapped in an ever-worsening downward spiral. Another is to accelerate investment in the infrastructure in order to preserve our largest industry and to leverage the competitive advantages bestowed by our natural resources.

There are two investment decisions that we need to make in a plan for Maine.

The first is whether to borrow at all, and this isn't really a close question. Borrowing for investments in Maine's infrastructure will help grow Maine's economy; if we don't make these investments, our economy simply is unlikely to grow in a meaningful way.

As I write in 2013, interest rates for state and municipal borrowing remain relatively low. Maine unfortunately missed the least expensive borrowing environment, but Maine remains in a good position to borrow in order to invest.

The second question, which is more complicated and poses more choices, is how Maine should secure a stream of revenues to pay back the debt we incur.

Consider roads and bridges. As cars become more fuel efficient, the state's revenues from the gasoline tax will continue to decline, even though the impacts on our roads from more miles being driven by more cars continue to climb. So, one option would be to increase the gasoline tax. Alternatively, Maine could impose a charge on each car tied to the number of miles driven in the previous year. Or we could impose user fees

– tolls – on our roads and bridges. It would be unwise, but we could fund debt repayment from general tax revenues. Or we could fashion a funding solution out of some combination of those alternatives.

We should be able to look to Maine's leaders to help us make these decisions about how to fund capital investments in Maine's critical assets,. Continuing political gamesmanship isn't helping. A growing economy will generate growing revenues to repay the new debt we incur. A dying economy won't generate enough revenue to pay even our existing debts – or to rescue our children from a bleak and unpromising future.

*   *   *

There is no place quite like Maine on the face of the earth. Look at us, and then look at the rest of the world. Our resources and our location make Maine different and give us huge competitive advantages and. Our surroundings – our mix of exciting cities and deeply rooted communities close by bountiful forests, farmlands, thousands of miles of coastline, rivers and lakes – constitute vital connective tissue that unites thousands of Mainers in abiding love for our state.

Our forests enable a paper and wood products industry that continues to grow in value, support lawyers in Portland and hospitals and doctors in Bangor, and attract millions of tourists to explore the North Woods and retirees to migrate to cities a short drive away.

Our Gulf of Maine coastline sustains tourism, lobstering, the Gulf of Maine fishery and boatbuilding – along with the coastal communities themselves, which are responsible for much of Maine's tourist economy.

The importance of leveraging Maine's competitive advantages should engage all Maine people and persuade us of the need to investing in the assets critical to maintaining those advantages. Pursuing a plan to strengthen and to grow the Maine economy needs to be our shared enterprise.

9
Stronger Democracy:
More Choice, Less Money

- Mainers value independence and good judgment, regardless of labels or party affiliation. Run-offs, open primaries or ranked choice voting will ensure that our elected leaders have the support of the majority of Maine people.

- We can't expect to have good outcomes – a sound plan and a growing economy – when the inputs are dysfunctional, inequitable and often corrupting. The flood of money in politics is alienating more and more of us from the political process and discouraging participation in it. We can...

  - Limit the extent to which big money and special interests dominate the political process through (1) a public match for small donations to political campaigns and (2) limiting campaign spending by political parties' "coordinated campaigns," SuperPACs and independent expenditure committees.

  - Make the sources of all money spent to influence elections fully transparent.

  - Break the link between campaign contributions and lobbyists' access to lawmakers by limiting the participation by lobbyists in fundraising for political campaigns.

Remember the beer that promised us "great taste, less filling?" Well, I believe our democracy in the 21st century should offer us more choice for less money. I believe in an open democracy with broad participation, and in the rule of law, not the rule of cash.

There's no question that fashioning a consensus plan to move Maine ahead will be a hard row to hoe. However, if we fix some of the biggest problems with the ways in which we choose our leaders and govern ourselves, we'll make it a whole lot more likely that our elected officials will work together to grow Maine's economy.

1. More Choice

Let's start with how we choose our leaders.

The political process belongs to all of us, not just to the two political parties and their well-financed allies on the left and the right. Our electoral processes should give us broad and good choices among candidates – choices that appeal not only to the few of us who stand on the left and right ends of the political spectrum, but also to most of us who occupy the center. Voters can have the kinds of choices that they want and deserve, and consensus at the end of the electoral process, if we have run-offs, open primaries or ranked choice voting.

Fewer and fewer Americans call themselves Republicans or Democrats these days. As recently as 2008, 39% of registered voters identified themselves as Democrats; that share had fallen to 31% by 2013. In 2008, 28% called themselves Republicans, but that number dwindled to 25% by June 2013.

Even fewer people are sufficiently party-affiliated to vote in their party primaries. The percentage of the nationwide voting age population who vote in Democratic primaries, for example, collapsed to 8% in 2010 from 21% in 1966.

In Maine in 2012 the Republican and Democratic Party candidates for the open U.S. Senate seat were each nominated in their respective party primaries with the votes of less than 2.5% of the state's registered voters, less than the population of the city of Sanford. Neither party candidate could have been said to have had a claim on a ballot position that was rooted in deep popular support.

The tenuous hold that the political parties have on Maine voters is even clearer in the state's gubernatorial general elections. In the last five general elections for governor, independents have won 38.1% of the votes, while Republicans have won 30.3% and Democrats 29.9%. During the gubernatorial elections over the past 43 years, Maine voters have elected independents in three of them.

The larger problem in Maine – overshadowing the decline of party affiliation – has been the repeated election of governors by less than a majority. Only on two occasions since 1970 has the Maine governor been elected by more than 50% of Maine voters.

Notwithstanding the declining allegiance they command from the electorate, however, the Democratic and Republican parties continue to exercise disproportionate political authority. In primaries and caucuses more and more dominated by big money and narrow interests, and in which fewer and fewer of us participate, Democrats and Republicans still nominate the so-called "major candidates" from whom we choose in our fall general elections. We even use tax dollars paid by all of us to hold primary elections in which 40% of us are excluded from voting.

Maine can fix these shortcomings simply and directly by changing our election laws to allow for an open primary, a run-off election between the top two vote getters in the general election or ranked choice voting. Either of these reforms would ensure that Maine's leaders would always be chosen by a majority of Maine voters.

2. Less Money and Less Risk of Corruption

We can't expect to have good outcomes – a sound plan and a growing economy – when the inputs are dysfunctional, inequitable and often corrupting.

The way we finance politics today has made both political parties smaller, narrower and more highly partisan, leading our legislature to behave like a parliament, where members *always* vote the party line and where compromise is a dirty word. Even "real solutions to big problems" that were endorsed by voters after vigorous campaigns become impossible to implement. It didn't used to be that way in way in Maine, and it doesn't need to be any longer.

The Supreme Court decision in the *Citizens United* case[31] opened the floodgates to excessive amounts of money in politics, and its most deeply dangerous impact has not been the anonymity and negativity of campaign attack ads, nor even the diminished and increasingly uncivil daily political dialogue, but rather what it has done to our political parties and to our legislative bodies.

Why did this happen? Well, when Willie Sutton was asked why he robbed banks, he said he did it because that's where the money is. Money has had the same effect on the parties.

Corporations, unions and incredibly wealthy individuals have found that their money can wield enormous, unregulated and anonymous influence in the post-*Citizens United* world. As a result, more and more political money has become narrow-purpose driven, often attached to foolish litmus tests like Grover Norquist's anti-tax pledge. Highly

---

[31] That case stands for the propositions that corporations are citizens with First Amendment rights and that unregulated spending by undisclosed corporations and individuals poses no significant danger to our political process.

ideological agendas have reshaped the political parties and positioned them on both narrower and shallower ground.

All of our electoral and legislating processes should be much more tightly insulated against the corrosion and corruption bred by uncontrolled and unregulated political money. Apart from the corruption of both politics and capitalism, the sheer force of money in politics today is alienating more and more Americans from the political process and discouraging participation in it.

While we wait for federal laws to change, we can battle back in Maine against the *Citizens United* decision and the unregulated excesses of money in politics by reinvigorating our Clean Elections program, by limiting in fair and constitutional ways the amounts of money that can be spent on election campaigns, by evening the playing field between small donors and big donors, by narrowing the ways in which political money can be raised by lobbyists and so-called "bundlers," and by making the origins of all money spent on campaigns fully transparent.

3. Break the Link

Voters need to be confident that the lawmakers whom they elect depend on them and make decisions that reflect their needs and concerns and not those of one or another set of special, narrow interests. When that confidence begins to break down, as it has in recent years, democracy is put at risk.

In a citizens' legislature like Maine's there is always the risk that lobbyists who represent special interests can gain excessive access to, if not also influence with, legislators (or governors or other elected officials) by providing money for their campaigns, either by raising (so-called "bundling") it and contributing it directly to the candidates' campaigns or contributing to the campaign effort through the "coordinated campaigns" of political parties, through SuperPACs or through "independent expenditure" committees.[32] It is ironic but revealing that the Foreign Corrupt Practices Act prohihits this kind of "pay to play" behavior in the case of American companies or citizens who seek to influence foreign lawmakers, with huge fines and prison terms visited upon

---

[32] The political parties' "coordinated campaigns," SuperPACs and "independent expenditure" committees are all legal vehicles for doing through other means what the law prohibits being done directly – influencing the outcome of elections with the spending of excessive and unlimited amounts of money from sources that are often hidden or are undisclosed. Corporations do it, unions do it and wealthy individuals do it. The most egregious of these are the "coordinated campaigns" of the political parties; they have an additional advantage over the SuperPACs and independent expenditure committees insofar as the parties' "coordinated campaigns" are permitted to coordinate their activities with the candidates, whereas the other two vehicles cannot do that.

those who are found to have violated the law... but "pay to play" is OK in Washington and Augusta.

Because many lobbyists are lawyers, the American Bar Association (ABA) has taken a special interest in the link between political contributions/campaign finance and lobbying. The authors of a 2011 ABA task force report wrote that "[t]he interplay of lobbying and the political money machine inevitably creates the potential for special interest influence and governmental decisions based on inappropriate criteria."[33]

The task force recommendation was blunt: "In order to dampen the risks of corruption and the appearance of corruption inherent in this situation, the Task Force favors measures that would largely separate these two spheres of political activity."[34] We can do that in Maine, and we should.

As we think about exactly how we should break the link between political money and lobbying in Maine, the proposed American Anti-Corruption Act[35] would be a good place to look for ideas. Drafted by Trevor Potter, former aide to Senator John McCain and former chairman of the Federal Elections Commission, and Larry Lessig, the Harvard Law School professor whose Ted Talk on the perils of the current political campaign finance practices[36] has won wide acclaim, the American Anti-Corruption Act "gets money out of politics so the people can get back in." All of its provisions might not be a good fit for Maine, but it points the way toward reforms that would reduce the influence of the flood of political money and would help restore to our politics and to our government in Maine the comity, cooperation and collaboration that once characterized it.

---

[33] "Lobbying Law in the Spotlight: Challenges and Proposed Improvements," http://www.americanbar.org/content/dam/aba/migrated/2011_build/administrative_law/lobbying_task_force_report_010311.authcheckdam.pdf, p.19.

[34] Id.

[35] www.anticorruptionact.org

[36] http://www.ted.com/talks/lawrence_lessig_we_the_people_and_the_republic_we_must_reclaim.html

10

Younger:
Turning Maine's Demographic Tide

- Unless Maine gets younger, our economy will not grow.

- Creating conditions that attract and retain young people will benefit Maine in every respect.

- Forgive Maine income tax liability for payments against student debt so long as a graduate lives and works in Maine for a prescribed length of time.

- Aggressively recruit educated and skilled legal immigrants to Maine.

Every piece of the plan discussed in the preceding chapters is targeted at making Maine younger. Why? Because it is the single most important challenge we have.

Unless Maine gets younger, our economy will not grow.

Unless Maine gets younger, we won't see new businesses, new farms and new opportunities.

Unless Maine gets younger, tax revenues – and services – will continue to decline.

Making Maine younger by holding onto our own young people and by seeking out skilled and educated young immigrants from other states and countries will balance and strengthen our economy, make us more competitive by lowering our *per capita* health care and education costs, help create jobs and position us for growth.

In some sectors of our economy, Maine already is getting younger; our growing population of new farmers, for example, is one of the youngest in America. We need to do more to accelerate this trend, to broaden it through more parts of our state's economy and even to reverse population declines in some of Maine's rural counties.

1. Invest in Young People Who Invest in Maine

We may not be able to compete with some of America's bigger and richer states to attract big auto and aircraft assembly plants; the table stakes – the price of the incentives – in those competitions are measured in the hundreds of millions of dollars. But Maine could compete in keeping at home and attracting from other areas both young people who want to start farms and businesses and the talent that current Maine employers need and that will help attract additional employers. Maine can offer an opportunity to be innovative and creative in surroundings that no other state can match.

Outstanding student loan balances in America now exceed $1 trillion, and graduating seniors leave college with average debt loads of more than $25,000. Maine now offers incentives for some graduates of Maine colleges – teachers, for example – to stay in Maine, but we can and should vastly broaden this program.

If a graduate between the ages of, say, 21 and 28 from *any* accredited two-year or four-year post-secondary school program stays in Maine or comes to Maine to work and to live – or to start a farm or a business – the state should forgive Maine income tax liability on a dollar for dollar basis for payments against student debt for so long as the graduate is living and working in Maine. We should be willing to bet that once they're here, have put down roots and experience life in Maine, they won't want to leave.

By offering to assist with repayments in graduates' early years, Maine could begin to rebalance our population. Over time a program like this would pay for itself, as active and employed young workers raise families, buy homes, pay taxes – and even start their own farms and businesses. It would be one step out of the downward vicious population cycle in which we are now trapped and towards a more virtuous cycle, one step toward a more competitive Maine.

2. Seek Out Skilled Immigrants

Maine also should be aggressively courting educated and skilled legal immigrants to our state, as Michigan and other states are doing.

My grandfather, Harry Epstein, was packed by his parents into steerage aboard a ship with other immigrants from eastern Europe in the late 1880's. Someone in his village in what is now Belarus had told him to go to Bangor when he got to North America.

The ship landed in Halifax, NS, and Harry found his way to Maine. He arrived in Bangor with no money, unable to speak English, with no obvious prospects for a job, much less a career, and very much alone. He was 12 years old.

Harry began his new life in America as a peddler, walking with a pack every week or so the long, dark and often bleak 95 miles from Bangor to Calais on what is now Route 9, the road we know as the Airline. He sold needles and thread and other dry goods to people who lived along the Airline, and a kind family in Bangor took him in and taught him English.

Harry became an American citizen in 1894, saved enough money to open a shop on Exchange Street, and married Ida in 1912. Even though his business failed during the Great Depression, Harry had saved some money and, with the help of scholarships, each of his three daughters was able to graduate from college and to obtain advanced degrees. One of them, Catherine Cutler, was my mother.

Harry Epstein's story is never far from my mind. It tells of his courage and of the significance of opportunity. It makes me proud of Bangor, of Maine and of America.

What may be most remarkable about Harry Epstein's story is how unremarkable a story it was. Mainers whose grandparents or great-grandparents came here from Ireland or Italy, Scotland or Quebec have similar stories about their immigrant grandparents and great-grandparents.

Immigrants historically have strengthened American communities and created jobs and wealth, and they could do that in Maine today. We just need to pursue skilled and educated immigrants with purpose and with vigor.

- 42% of all doctorate-level science and engineering workers in America today *are* foreign-born.

- 25% of all high-tech firms founded in the United States between 1995 and 2005, including an astonishing 52% of all Silicon Valley firms, had at least one foreign-born founder. By 2005, the companies that they founded employed 450,000 workers and generated over $50 billion in sales.

- 40% of the Fortune 500 companies were founded by immigrants or by the children of immigrants.

- Immigrant graduates who stay in America mean more jobs for native-born Americans, not fewer. At Microsoft, for example, for every immigrant who is hired, four non-immigrants are hired.

New evidence in many regions demonstrates the positive impacts of immigrants, including growth in population, decline in crime, neighborhoods being revitalized and small towns coming back to life.

A smarter approach to immigration is critically important for the State of Maine. Maine lags the rest of New England and much of America in educational attainment and R & D activity, two of the principal ingredients for economic growth and jobs. We need young, talented, educated, job-creating immigrants just as much as they need the opportunities that Maine provided to my grandfather and to so many others.

Here are a few of the steps that Maine can take to attract that talent... and to get younger in the process:

- Collaborate with Maine educational and research institutions, employers and the congressional delegation to maximize Maine's allotment of H1b visas;

- Organize Maine counties, towns and businesses to cooperate in the creation of EB-5 investment opportunities; and,

- Actively recruit foreign researchers for the University of Maine and University of New England graduate schools and for our biomedical and other research centers.

11
Set a Bold Course Forward

- Now is the time to unshackle ourselves from the legacy of poor decisions and needless conflict. Maine people deserve better.

- A good plan for Maine will reflect our most important values: fairness, compassion for our neighbors, shared obligations to each other and to our natural environment, and a rational, balanced approach to solving problems.

Maine in 2013 stands on a knife edge – at once on the precarious edge of further decline driven by worsening demographics, but also on the cusp of extraordinary economic opportunities not seen in Maine since perhaps the late 19th century.

If we don't now set our sights on a vision of what Maine can be, and a set of goals and a strategy that will get us there, we will have consigned our children and grandchildren – if they remain in Maine at all – to a future of mediocre prospects, simply because we have grown accustomed to a *status quo* defined by low expectations.

Now is the time to act, and to act boldly. We don't have a lot of time, but we have enough. We have just enough time to develop a plan that leverages our assets and advantages, protects and creates opportunity, sparks economic activity and growth, and builds a strong foundation for Maine's future.

If Maine people embrace a plan and elect leaders worthy of this marvelous place that we call home, there is no challenge we won't overcome.

We will become healthier, smarter, stronger, younger and more prosperous. Our economy will grow. Our children will come home to Maine and raise their families here. We will be able to provide both for ourselves and for the needy and vulnerable among us.

This book doesn't pretend to offer a fully developed plan for Maine. It is, rather, a starting point based on my love for this state and a vision for what it can be.

If a reader walked away from perusing this small volume with but one conclusion, I would want it to be simply this: Maine needs a plan, a good one, and we have it in our power to create one.

A plan for Maine won't be widely embraced if it is seen to be partisan – a Democratic or Republican plan – or if it advantages one part of Maine or another. A good plan will place the interests of the State of Maine over those of one or another political party and the interest groups that support it, and will acknowledge the fact that the various parts of Maine depend upon each other.

A good plan for Maine will be realistic, responsible and will leverage our competitive strengths.

A good plan for Maine will reflect the most important Maine values: fairness, compassion for our neighbors, shared obligations to each other and to our natural environment, and a rational, balanced approach to solving problems.

As we set forth together on the process of developing a shared vision and plan for Maine, permit me to suggest three resolutions to guide us in our quest.

First, each of us would do well to spend at least a little bit of time thinking about the social contract that binds us together – about what my Republican friend called "the parable of the Good Samaritan and its moral analogs" – about the growing inequities that no political palaver can hide, about Maine's bedrock values of fairness and opportunity and how those are often ill-served today.

Perhaps you'll conclude, as I have, that great value remains in notions of common goals and mutual enterprise, where burdens, obligations and rewards are fairly shared, and that government policies ought to enable, not inhibit, real opportunities for each of us to make the most of our respective talents and ought to encourage us to pursue those opportunities.

Second, it is time to talk seriously about the role of government and to acknowledge the importance of positive, forward-looking leadership, strategic vision and planning.

Voters deserve to be treated like grownups. They should be engaged by their leaders in serious conversations about taxes and spending; about the differences between government's annual operating expenses and long-term investments in their children's futures; about immigration, health care, education and all of the other complicated public issues that affect their lives.

We should expect from our elected officials a sound understanding of what needs to be fixed. We should expect and demand creative thinking about reforms that will lift old burdens and not impose new ones, that will release energies and not sap enthusiasm, that will attract and retain human talent, and that both will create opportunity and incite the will and determination to pursue it.

Third, we all need to pay better attention to our words and behavior in public discussion and debate. Words can inspire and heal, or they can hurt and inflame. We should never excuse repeated and intentional distortions of the facts, bullying behavior and slanderous remarks about good people.

Our leaders should demonstrate both the intention and the ability to draw from us the best that is in each of us, to unite us, and to engender trust among us. We should expect our leaders to have a clear understanding of the world in which we live and compete, the skills and the grace to represent us well in that world, and the ability to guide us in ways that will make our great state better for our having lived here.

One of the things about Maine that sets us apart from other states is how we Mainers feel about each other and about our state. We are deeply loyal to our friends and neighbors, and we love our corner of America with an intensity that most folks "from away" can't fully grasp. We all want to live out our lives in Maine, and we want our kids to be able to live and work here, too.

Whether we operate a B&B near Bethel, haul lobster traps off Stonington, work in a sawmill in Searsmont, grow potatoes or broccoli in the County, are part of Portland's art scene or haul logs in Piscataquis or Somerset County... we're one state, one community, and we're in this together.

At a time when our state seems divided, when our economy is stuck and when our politics are broken, the best remedy is not to keep doing things the same way, hoping the results will be different; rather, the path forward lies in working together toward serious political and economic reform.

Let's reject the skeptics and naysayers, the partisans and the narrow interests, the timid and the selfish.

Let's not allow the Lost Decade to become Maine's default setting.

Let's hit the "reset" button on our expectations.

Let's together embrace a belief in the fundamental strengths of Maine and her people, a vision of a future full of opportunity, a plan and a strategy to overcome our challenges and to capitalize on our advantages.

Let's set a bold course forward toward a healthier, smarter, stronger, younger and more prosperous State of Maine.

About the Author

Throughout a distinguished career that has taken him from his hometown of Bangor to the nation's capital, around the world and home again to Maine, Eliot Cutler has maintained an abiding love for his state and a commitment to helping Maine fulfill its promise as a place of unrivaled natural beauty and boundless opportunity. A lawyer, public servant, and successful business-man, Cutler has earned a reputation as a visionary leader, passionate advocate and pragmatic problem-solver.

In the 2010 race for Governor, where Cutler went from a political unknown to within little more than a percentage point of defeating frontrunner Paul LePage, he was endorsed by virtually every major newspaper in Maine.

The state's largest daily newspaper said Cutler was the one candidate who "has the potential to bridge philosophical divides, heal political wounds and conquer daunting problems that are confronting state government and Maine's overburdened taxpayers." Another leading newspaper said that "Eliot Cutler is the only candidate with the vision and skills to match Maine's challenges."

As a public servant, Cutler helped craft America's foundational environmental laws and managed the policies and budgets of federal energy, natural resources, science and environmental agencies.

As a strategist and lawyer for governments, business corporations and citizens groups, Cutler helped clients grapple with worldwide legal and public policy problems during a career in three law firms and two countries that spanned more than 35 years.

As an active entrepreneur, businessman and investor, Cutler has helped start and manage successful businesses, served on the boards of directors of private and public companies and advised and managed private and public philanthropic organizations.

Eliot Cutler is a graduate of Harvard College and the law school of Georgetown University, He is 67 and has been married for 40 years to Melanie Stewart Cutler, M.D. The Cutlers live in Cape Elizabeth, Maine. Eliot and Melanie have two children, Abigail Cutler and Zachary Cutler.